"Eileen Morgan does an excellent job of mapping the course for navigating the previously uncharted global ethical waters. By identifying best practices, she leads the reader on a journey from Surviving, to Understanding to Knowing the ethical issues that frequently confront international business people. This is a must read for anyone who wants to successfully compete in world markets."

–Michael J. Litwin, Executive Vice President, Chief Credit Officer, Heller Financial, Inc.

"Eileen Morgan has combined the pragmatic concerns of the individual manager with the moral concerns that come from personal-life history, cultural roots, and corporate ethical culture . . . This book focuses on the constructive task of formulating and using an "ethical map," and is sure to be a tonic to conscientious managers who want to navigate cross-cultural commerce with integrity. It has done a superb job of creating order out of the complexity of cross-cultural moral experience by insisting that the complexity must be honored and appropriated rather than ignored or suppressed."

–Dr. Richard Beauchamp, Professor of Ethics, Christopher Newport University

"In this groundbreaking book, Eileen Morgan has provided scores of real-life examples and developed a framework for approaching ethical leadership in international business. This is mandatory reading for anyone involved in global management today . . . This is an important book on an important subject."

–Stephen H. Rhinesmith, Ph.D., Author, *A Manager's Guide to Globalization*

"Eileen Morgan provides us with a much needed roadmap for how to walk the path of ethical leadership with practical feet. She reminds us that ethical decision-making is a critical aspect of every day leadership, and that we can all choose to be 'ethical pioneers' in our companies and our communities. Every leader engaged in global business can benefit from the lessons and stories included in this book."

–**Christi A. Olson,** Ph.D. Chair, Telecommunications Management Department, Golden Gate University

"Eileen Morgan's thoughtful analysis of 'ethical capital' should be read by anyone who does business in a global environment . . . Morgan's book presents the issue clearly, comprehensively and compellingly, demonstrating that ethics is an indispensable aspect of individual leadership and organizational credibility. . . . It provides a clear roadmap for business leaders who need to communicate their commitment to integrity and accountability to their employees, their partners, and their customer, making their 'ethical capital' one of their most valuable assets."

–**Nell Minnow,** Principal, Lens, The Corporate Governance Investors

"Eileen Morgan gives excellent insight into ethical practices. She focuses on business but her insights have general application. This book also describes differences in ethical interpretation that can arise between diverse cultures. Ms. Morgan has made an excellent contribution to understanding the benefit of positive ethical practices."

–**David C. Lincoln,** Sponsor, Lincoln Center for Applied Ethics, College of Business, Arizona State University; President, Arizona Oxides, LLC

Navigating
Cross-Cultural Ethics

Navigating
Cross-Cultural Ethics:

What Global Managers Do Right to Keep from Going Wrong

EILEEN MORGAN

Boston, Oxford, Johannesburg, Melbourne, New Delhi, Singapore

Library of Congress Cataloging-in-Publication Data

Morgan, Eileen, 1949–
    Navigating cross-cultural ethics : what global managers do right to keep from going wrong / by Eileen Morgan.
        p.   cm.
    Includes bibliographical references and index.
    ISBN 0-7506-9915-9 (alk. paper)
    1. Business ethics.   2. International business enterprises—Moral and ethical aspects.   I. Title.
HF5387.M655   1998
174'.4—dc21   98-37850
                                                                              CIP

British Library Cataloguing-in-Publication Data
A catalogue record for this book is available from the British Library.

The publisher offers special discounts on bulk orders of this book.
For information, please contact:
Manager of Special Sales
Butterworth-Heinemann
225 Wildwood Avenue
Woburn, MA 01801-2041
Tel: 781-904-2500
Fax: 781-904-2620

For information on all Butterworth–Heinemann publications available, contact our World Wide Web home page at: http://www.bh.com

10 9 8 7 6 5 4 3 2 1

Printed in the United States of America

Epigraph

ETHICS:\e-thiks\n. sing. or pl.

1. A discipline dealing with good and evil and with moral duty
2. Moral principles or practice

Dedication

For Keith, who makes everything possible

Table of Contents

Preface

Ethics is a tricky subject to talk about. We often feel safe talking about ethics when we frame the conversation in philosophy, values, and codes. This is the level that my southern grandmother would have called "good preaching," or what the preacher in her small Southern Baptist Church was doing when he was talking about what she considered other people's shortcomings. However, when the preacher railed about shortcomings which she could rightfully ascribe to herself, she would huffily pronounce, "Now he's quit preaching and gone to meddlin'!"

This book is about "meddlin'." It is intended to meddle in the lives of managers and leaders and the obligation they must passionately develop towards understanding ethical dynamics in their organizations. It is intended to meddle in the day-to-day lives of leaders who are learning how to build ethical capacity in those organizations. It's an attempt to move the dialogue about cross-cultural ethics from the universals of "global values," philosophical perspectives, and corporate ethics codes on brass plaques in marble lobbies, to the day-to-day uncertainties of individual predicaments and decision-making.

There are stories from many individuals in many companies represented in this book to whom I am indebted. These voices have been heard over fifteen years as I worked as an organizational consultant around the world. Other voices and stories were heard through individual interviews as I went about learning what the specific experiences in ethical dilemmas and decision-making felt and sounded like.

One of the surprises I had in writing this book is that at the same time more companies are crafting ethics codes, providing ethics training, and hiring ethics officers, there is still a deep reluctance on the part of individuals at all levels to discuss their stories for attribution—even when the stories reflect positive values and behaviors. Hence, while many voices informed the ideas upon which this book is founded, relatively few felt free to be identified and heard for attribution. This, as much as anything else about these chapters, is a telling indicator of how a veil of silence still descends over this topic, particularly at the individual level. It is a potent reminder about how far global companies have to go before we and they can grapple with these complexities in a meaningful and truth-telling way.

Business ethics engages us in a deeply personal way because it is a powerful and unique entry point—the conscience and spirit of a single human being—into the large, seemingly impersonal organization. It is our stake in the ground which allows us to see ourselves in the mirror we call our organization, as well as the larger mirrors of other cultures—the ultimate reflectors of ourselves. We can look closely and ask, "Is our reflection there? Is it clear? Do I exist in all my humanness, with my hopes, my fears, and doubts?"

This book is about the personal reflection that the subject of business and ethics provides in global companies, and also about the role of reflective business practice for the leader, the manager, the employee. It is about putting aside all our previous excuses for tackling this issue head-on. It is about jettisoning our zero-sum mentality regarding corporate ethics, our win-lose philosophy. The very act of reading this book revokes your license to shrug, throw up your hands and say, "It's all so complex!" It is. And you must—absolutely must—deal with the issues of business and ethics in complex global organizations anyway, with caring, with intentionality, and with intelligence. My deepest hope is that this book will help you do just that.

Acknowledgments

There are people I wish to acknowledge who are responsible for helping make this book a reality. Particularly, there are managers around the globe who engaged me—and continue to engage me—in deep, personal dialogue about their experiences. There are colleagues in my field and my universe of practice who listened patiently to my ideas and extroverted ramblings and who helped bring some order and coherence to them. I am grateful that these friends and colleagues steered me toward colleagues of theirs, colleagues who added enormous value to my thinking and writing and who allowed me to understand their lifeworld as they struggle with ethical dilemmas everyday in their work.

Good friends and colleagues Meg Hartzler, Gruffie Clough, Ron Gager, Gwen Kennedy, Christi Olson, Paula Singer, and Carolyn Lejuste provided endless hours of patient listening and critical feedback. Dr. Matt Hamabata of The Fielding Institute provided ideas and insights very early on that added enormous value in my thinking, triggering intuitive leaps and connections and helping me arrive at clarity through his laser like questions.

There are others in the academic and professional fields of business and ethics I'd like to acknowledge who influenced my thinking, such as Dr. Thomas Donaldson from The Wharton School, Dr. Peter Vaill from St. Thomas University, and Dr. Richard Beauchamp, Ethics Professor at Christopher Newport University, who was a wonderful sounding board for my ideas and who encouraged me mightily at critical junctions during the process.

It's at times like these that family members shine in wonderful and unexpected ways. Many thanks to my sister-in-law, Patti Jones Morgan, for her assistance with setting up and following up on interviews, and to my brother Michael for his technical help and the sharing of colleagues.

I also wish to thank Meg Wheatley who has helped me learn how to write from the heart as well as with spirit, and who has been a close friend, even though separated by miles.

I particularly wish to thank Karen Speerstra, Publishing Director of Butterworth-Heinemann, who was enthusiastic about this endeavor and knew that it would be born "when it was ready to be born." Thank you, Karen, and to Rita Lombard, the ever capable assistant who actually made the book a physical reality.

There are a few others who helped me believe in what I had to say, even when I had convinced myself otherwise. The first of these are the members of The Sturbridge Group—Mary Lou Michael, Judith Ward, Raymond Madsen, and Tamara Bliss—who not only helped shape the voice of the book, but who simply refused to let me quit when I thought that was the right thing to do.

The second is Matt Kayhoe, my consulting partner and friend who spent many, many hours listening to my initial ramblings and then rolled up his sleeves to work with me to help make this idea "something" instead of just a passionate idea.

Finally (and firstly, as well), there is my life partner Keith Melville who has inspired me to write since the first hour I knew him. Thank you for being my partner, friend, and editor. Thank you also for the continuous supply of inspiration and support, and for the good care and feeding you provided to your fellow writer when she was deep in her frenzy of deadlines. You were there at the difficult times saying all the right things and helping in all the right ways. I am deeply happy and grateful to share my life with you.

Chapter 1

Scanning for Dragons

"Ethics is a barrel of worms."

... REP. OMAR BURLESON (D-TEX.)

I was sitting in a meeting in Moscow recently, working with a Fortune 100 company. A large group of Russian, Ukrainian, and American managers were trying to work through some of the communication and operational difficulties they encountered in trying to put together joint ventures in several types of businesses. I had been working in Russia with several clients on a variety of projects since the beginning of perestroika and had recently published a book, co-authored with a Russian psychologist, on the topic of sociocultural barriers that hindered Russians and Americans in working together. Many of the issues being discussed, both rationally and quite emotionally, were issues with which I was familiar first hand.

My Russian colleague in the room was at that time director of the International Business School of Moscow, a new type of institution that seemed to be sprouting up in Moscow as rapidly as the fast food chains that had begun to appear in the ancient streets of the Arbat and Red Square. Every Russian I met in those days described himself as a "biznez" man. The Russians have no word of their own that accurately describes the dynamics of free market trade and capitalism. Until those chaotic,

1

heady days of revolution, the very word *biznez* was the lowest of
epithets, flung in the face of an adversary at the emotional fever
pitch of an argument. It was shorthand communication, imply-
ing that the party on the other end of the insult was utterly corrupt, and wholly unredeemable.

Andrei, my colleague in this session, was cut from a different cloth. The program he directed, the International Business
School of Moscow, was a product of the Ministry of Trade training school aimed at the elite corp of Russians picked to engage in
trade and diplomacy outside the old Soviet Union. It had recently been named as the leading choice among Russian business
schools by the *Wall Street Journal*, a highly coveted recommenda-
tion at a time when many former Russian entities were relabeling
themselves as *biznez* schools. Andrei, trained in the west in business practices, was now a lecturer every summer at the Harvard
Business School and the University of Virginia Darden School
of Business. He traveled frequently and freely in the west,
particularly the United States. He was intelligent, articulate, and
engaging.

We had been asked to speak together during one of the sessions. I spoke about the "baggage" (the mindsets, assumptions,
and cultural and business orientations) that Americans bring
when working with Russians. Andrei spoke about the "baggage" Russians bring when working with Americans. At this
particular moment he was speaking about the Culture of Corruption, a term he had coined, a culture embedded in the very
fabric of the Russian culture. He suggested plainly, even off-
handedly, that Americans and other westerners must expect that
whomever they are dealing with in Russia is, or would be, on
some level, corrupt. "I have engaged in it," he stated casually.
"We all have. It's a fact of life here." Having spent time before in
Russia working with government ministries and their officials, I
had a good sense of what Andrei was trying to convey, and I
was not particularly surprised by it. I had come up against the
types of behavior used to make something happen in Russia, behaviors that seem questionable, inconvenient, or even nonsensi-
cal at times. Andrei's seemingly straightforward comments,

however, had a decidedly different effect on the other American managers.

The room erupted with angry comments and questions. "How can you possibly say that?" said one American woman who was quite agitated. "That's just not true!" denied another man, as angry Americans took exception to Andrei's comments. They had met, the Americans stressed, many helpful, good, caring people in Russia who were not corrupt.

Andrei tried to explain what he was saying to help them understand what was happening in their business interactions so they could understand and learn how to deal with the consistent undercurrents of corruption. The session ended in bedlam. A hasty break was called to calm tempers with some strong Russian tea.

As I sat there thinking about the scene I had just witnessed, I began to suspect that the Americans were upset about the casual way in which Andrei talked about corruption as a way of life, as if he didn't think it was such a terrible thing in itself. The Americans were obviously personalizing to actual individuals they knew or had met the behaviors about which he spoke. They did not seem able to reconcile the two sets of information being presented: the individuals they knew personally and his flat assertion that all Russians were part of a Culture of Corruption.

For 15 years I have worked as an organizational consultant in large companies, many of them with international groups and clients. I am used to the struggles that groups go through to be heard and understood as they try to communicate across boundaries of geography and culture. But something different was going on. Americans were trying to persuade a Russian that what he was saying about corruption and ethics from his own cultural point of view was not accurate.

They were saying these things at the same time that some Americans were complaining bitterly that unlike their competition with whom they went head to head everyday, they were not allowed to pay any bribes (or "permissions" or "facilitating payments") to the local manufacturers to win the contracts to get their airplane engines and locomotives built on site from imported U.S. components. They were not allowed to do this, they said, because of the company's strictly enforced ethics policy. They were, they stated resentfully, forced to walk away from the table and turn these lucrative deals right into the hands of their competitors, who apparently were not hamstrung by strict corporate ethical policies. They certainly did not want to behave unethically themselves, they reassured me, but they were clearly angry and distressed by this conflict: the conflict between doing business and making profits—what they had been sent here to do—and the company's ethics policies, which prevented them from doing what was necessary to function in Russia.

As I sat in my chair on the dais watching the agitated clusters of company representatives file out of the room, I thought about other instances in which I had felt the tension of individuals charged with conducting business overseas profitably but faced with obstacles in conducting it ethically. Logistical and administrative transactions that Americans take for granted in getting through the day became moments of truth. Merely trying to get packages or parts delivered, paperwork completed, and staff recruited, hired, and trained could generate the "oh-oh" feeling (a wonderfully useful and descriptive phrase taught to me by a friend who teaches self-defense to children). Whether it was dealing with banks and agent organizations in Cairo while developing a new Suez canal toll payment product or faced with parts delivery problems in which "a small favor" (like finding a job for the niece of the local customs agent) could go a long way toward expediting the transaction, I learned to recognize the cost of transgressing ethical norms and the cost, both real and perceived, of staying within them.

When it comes to running a business in another culture—or with suppliers, vendors, or customers from other cultures—the simple rules for getting things done, with which we in the United States are familiar, simply don't always apply. The very process that we define as "getting things done" looks different in Moscow, Madras, or Milan than it does in Milwaukee or Mobile. Straightforward business transactions such as placing orders, shipping goods, generating documentation, or socializing with customers become colored by different ideas about accomplishing business or the importance of interpersonal and long standing relationships. The confusion and emotion around ethics in cross-cultural transactions was evident in the room with the Russians, Ukrainians, and Americans. I have heard similar expressions of confusion and frustration while working with managers in India (both Indian and U.S. managers) and Latin America. In management courses at some of the leading corporate management education institutions in the world, the ethical dilemmas of doing business across cultures frequently come up.

WHAT ARE WE TALKING ABOUT WHEN WE TALK ABOUT BUSINESS ETHICS?

The tension between how we know we *ought* to behave as individuals and corporate citizens and *what actually goes on* in day to day practice is clearly illustrated by the level of cynicism and dark humor that accompanies the topic. As managers and citizens we shake our heads at the practices of some high-profile investment traders, both here and around the world, who are responsible for stealing millions of investors' dollars. We are enraged at oil conglomerates trying to walk away from accountability and billions of dollars of damages caused by mismanaged vessels. We are appalled at careless disregard for human life and safety in countries where the regulations that exist are not enforced strictly or at all. We decry the national scale of corruption evident in stories coming from Italy, India, and Malaysia. It only takes reading the newspapers to understand the personal and organizational tension that exists around ethics.

The subversive chief social commentators of our day, the cartoonists, hit the subject regularly and with deadly accuracy. Scott Adams, creator of the brilliant and wildly popular comic strip *Dilbert*, zeroes in on the commonly dismissive notion of business ethics being "mostly common sense."

Gary Trudeau, creator of the long running *Doonesbury* strip, regularly skewers the ethical practices of Wall Street, focusing, as do Bill Rechin and Don Wilder in their strip *Crock*. Rechin and

Figure 1.1 Dilbert 9/1/96 reprinted by permission of United Feature Syndicate, Inc.

Wilder also contend in their strip that the convenient although cynical working definition of ethics is "Right is what you can get away with. Wrong is what you can't."

It is easy to stay cynical, to throw our hands up in the air or shrug our shoulders and sigh resignedly that it's all too complex. It is easier to give in to our "inner cynic"and say that *business ethics* is an oxymoron. The kind of dismissive attitude that conveys "We're all in this together and ain't it awful," is easier,

Figure 1.2 Crock Cartoon 8/6/87 *Right Is What You Can Get Away With.* Reprinted with special permission of North American Syndicate.

but it's no longer responsible or smart. This book is about why managers can no longer afford that dismissive attitude and what they can do to change that attitude in their company.

What Is the "It" We Are Trying to Get Away With?

Albert Z. Carr, in his now famous *Harvard Business Review* article "Is Business Bluffing Ethical?" (1968) suggested that if business is nothing more than a game, as many of its players insist, then business ethics are simply the sleights of hand and bluffing techniques that go along with knowing the rules of any game, such as poker. One must be able to divorce one's personal morality from what is right and wrong to win the game.

Trying to reach a working definition of business ethics becomes even more of a challenge when we place it in the global crossfire of values, judgments, and agreements about what is morally right behavior. The age-old question, "Whose values?" surfaces again—and often. One of the things that clouds our ability to speak clearly about business ethics is that we try to cover a vast territory of meanings, attitudes, philosophies, values, and behavior with just one word, *ethics*, not unlike what we have been trying to get away with for centuries by using the single word *love* to convey a spectrum of meanings, acts, and relationships.

Very recently I worked with The Chautauqua Institution, this country's oldest institution for adult education, moderating a weeklong series of dialogues and discussions under the title *The Business and Ethics Forum*. On each of four days, staff, managers, and sometimes union representatives of a well-known company were invited to discuss with an audience of 200 people an ethical dilemma of their choosing they had faced or were facing. These ethical dilemmas were presented as "live cases" in which the individuals from the company who were actually involved in the situation presented the situation to the participating audience. Each live case was presented from the perspectives of the shareholder, the organization, the community, the union, and other groups in the company who were affected by the situation. After a brief presentation of the dilemma, as defined by the company, from the perspectives of management, employee, shareholder, and community, the audience was invited to think through the same issues in small groups and react to the company representatives with questions, challenges, and issues. The discussion was lively, passionate, intelligent, emotional, and frequently loud. Underlying each company's discussion each day was the wide array of topics that were considered ethical dilemmas. None of these dilemmas specifically addressed issues in doing business globally, so the reader can see how difficult it is to talk about these issues, even in the context of our own culture. Here's a look at the spectrum that emerged. (Each company that participated in the forum requested its name be held confidential. I found this to be true of many individuals with whom I spoke.)

"Look What You're Doing to Us"

Located in a small upstate New York town, it was clear to Glassco, Inc., that the future of the business lay in investing heavily in its fiber optics business, which was growing tenfold, and away from the classic consumer products business for which the company was known by name worldwide. In the town of 30,000 that was home to corporate headquarters, the company employed 10,000 persons. Fully 10 percent of the company's employees worldwide were employed in the consumer products business. Whereas the company had made a commitment to build the new fiber optics plant in the same town as the corporate headquarters, the talent required in this high-tech business would not be readily available from the town. It was clear that jobs being lost in the consumer end of the business would not be replaced by townspeople in the new fiber optics business.

THE ETHICAL DILEMMA: Is it ethical for a company to change its line of business so completely that it is has a dramatic effect on the small community to whom it has provided jobs, livelihood, and millions of dollars in community resources?

"You Have No Right to Do That!"

The second day's ethical dilemma was presented jointly by the plant manager and union president of Truckcom, an international automotive company. This small rural company had been the target of five takeovers in 4 years and was still losing money. The company was heavily unionized and had most recently come under non-U.S. management. The new management felt hamstrung by its inability to work through the issues necessary for revitalization and productivity. The union contract prohibited the new management from hiring outside the company for the skills and talent they believed they needed. In an eleventh-hour rescue, the foreign management team decided to leave the plant open but to set aside the union agreement and its hiring restrictions. Over the course of a few years, the plant has returned to financial health and today employs almost 200 persons in a small town desperate for work. But the company did it without a union contract. As the plant manager and union president described the history to the audience, they presented the dilemma from the multiple viewpoints of management, union, and the community. It was evident that many sensitivities still exist throughout the community and that this chapter in the town's history will not be forgotten easily, even though the financial prospects of many individuals in the town increased.

THE ETHICAL DILEMMA: Is it ethical for the leadership of a company to violate and disregard a contract struck in good faith between workers and management, even if doing so means the survival of an industry crucial to the health of the community?

"A Faustian Bargain"

The third company in the *Business and Ethics Forum* was a manufacturing division of a global conglomerate, Transport, Inc.. This company is renowned for its progressive management practices, which contribute greatly to its stunning successful financial performance worldwide in every one of the leading businesses and industries in which it competes. The company is big. It is relentlessly demanding in its standards for productivity, quality, and work performance. It is a very "lean"company, so much so that almost everyone complains of being stretched to the breaking point, only to find a new set of higher standards and goals. Sixty-hour weeks are routine. In this company there is no question about making business goals. They are made. The company prides itself on having "the most valuable jobs in the world" and openly manages the entire workforce so that only the very best of the very best can work there. But if you do work there, you do so with your eyes wide open as the result of a perfectly clear choice. As the human resources manager who helped set up this company's live case explained:

> Everyone knows what the deal is when they accept a job. We are very clear about the demands, the hours, the expectations, the pressure. It is also very clear to people we hire that they are joining the most productive company in the world, and there are huge payoffs for that. We pay more than other companies. We have fantastic benefits. They have an opportunity to work for one of the best companies in the world. But that opportunity has a price tag on it both in terms of pressure as well as expectations.

And what is one of the benefits for the larger good as a result of all this productivity and effectiveness? The company recently donated $1 million to a local high school in a depressed part of the community for an entire refurbishing. "We wouldn't be able to make those kinds of contributions unless we had the kind of productivity that we have. We can make these kinds of demands because we are who we are."

THE ETHICAL DILEMMA: Is it ethical for a company to make the kind of professional contract with its workers that strains their professional and personal stamina, offers no job security beyond "today," yet rewards them handsomely, simply because they are big enough and profitable enough and they can?

"Does Having a Playbook Help?"

The last company to participate in a dialogue on ethical issues in business used its experiences in an increasingly international arena to focus on its ethical dilemmas. This company began as a large family-owned manufacturing business. Its Midwest roots and values have served it well over the almost 100 years it has been in business. The company was founded on a strong sense of ethical behavior that employees have always considered a hallmark, and about which the company is genuinely proud. Over the past several decades this company has become increasingly global in suppliers, manufacturing plants, and markets. Along with that globalization has come situations that often run counter to the values and beliefs on which the company was founded. Managers find themselves in situations in which their own sense of personal values derived from deeply embedded American values conflict with the day-to-day values of relationships and doing business in other cultures. In one story, a talented woman manager was told not to participate in an important meeting with a Middle Eastern client because it was assumed the client would not deal with her and it would make the company look bad. When this manufacturing company decided it was time to develop a code of ethics for everyone in the company, many took exception. It would be an insult, they felt, to write down these deeply held beliefs, an insinuation that everyone didn't know what these values were or how to conduct themselves.

THE ETHICAL DILEMMA: Is it ethical to insult our own employees by codifying our values and operating principles, even if it is for the good of the company in the long run?

Listening to the dialogue around business and ethics during the live case discussions in each of the company sessions at Chautauqua, it was easy to see how personal values, legal opinions both informed and uninformed, and cultural values and preferences all mixed together to produce a confusing stew of what is considered ethical behavior. Passion and personal values mix interchangeably with preference and performance, and stumble clumsily toward an attempt at consensus and understanding.

Corporate leadership historically has left the language of ethics to the moral philosophers, who while providing critically needed conceptual foundations, typically fail to construct a useful bridge to managers and individuals engaged in day-to-day combat on the line. To confuse the issue even more, many of our best management thinkers and moral philosophers have conflicting definitions of what business ethics means. What we have been working with so far includes, "the application of moral values" (Wines and Napier 1992), "the activity of applying moral precepts to concrete problems" (Churchill 1982), "relating business activities to some concept of human good and evaluating business practices" (Donaldson 1989), "the interaction of business and ethics" (DeGeorge 1987), and the rules, standards, codes or principles that provide guidelines for morally right behavior and truthfulness in specific situations (Abratt, Hel, and Higgs 1992). Some refer to business ethics as a "study"(Barry 1985).

What's missing from the realm of business and ethics is clear, practical language that speaks to the manager and provides practical guidance. It is timely to develop a working definition that makes sense to the global manager, and it is imperative in this time of increasing organizational complexity. If managers are to move from disempowered cynicism to empowered ethical leadership, it is imperative they be given the tools to implement the transition.

This book is for managers who are interested in moving beyond the MBA classroom aspects of business and ethics and into the day-to-day world of application. Because this book will help managers in day-to-day business transactions, the focus on business ethics is not just from the "moral" point of view, but from the total perspective of individual managers and their values, the policies and codes in place from a corporate point of view, and the internal structural and process-oriented systems that keep the whole game in progress.

One of the reasons for the confusion in our language about business and ethics is that we talk simultaneously about three levels of ethical interaction as if they were all the same. The following takes a look at how these levels are different and why it is important to know the difference.

We need to understand the fundamental differences among the labels of personal values, corporate values, and social responsibility when describing business behaviors to think clearly about ethical conflicts and dilemmas. Understanding these labels gives managers clearer choices for working through ethical conflicts as individuals in the organization. When I am talking with managers about business and ethics, the conversation includes dilemmas relating to environmental policies in Trinidad, child labor practices in Korea, accepting bribes to get customs shipments through customs, and padding expense accounts as a means of supplementing income—sometimes all in the same conversation. These are different types of behaviors. Some involve individual judgment, some involve corporate policies, and some involve personal values. In our human desire for clarity and our yearning for predictability, we attempt to put ethical actions into clear, distinct, easily labeled buckets. This book recognizes that this is a paradox regarding business and ethics that we do not usually deal with, this notion of understanding the pieces but appreciating them as a whole. Although leaders have to learn to differentiate behaviors to build ethical competence in organizations as leaders, as always in this complex world, nothing acts alone. We all interact with each other. As managers we need to understand the differences to understand how they are part of a whole.

Carr's point of view about business ethics starts from the personal perspective of the individual, and many people argue that understanding the world of business ethics begins at the individual level. Individual integrity is unquestionably at the heart of the attitudes, philosophies, and decisions in which many managers today find themselves engaged. The notion of individual accountability and responsibility is at the very core of our western philosophy of right and wrong, as explored in Chapter 4. It is an essential beginning point. When we try to wrestle the hydra-headed dragon of business ethics in a global context, however, talking about personal values simply is not enough.

For years, salespeople from a large plastics company were expected to go to concubine houses with their customers in Japan, and they did it. Today, however, these salespeople are more verbal about their discomfort about the practice, and they simply refuse to go. The old fears about not playing along with the customer have given way to a greater degree of comfort among these salespeople living out their personal values.

Over the last few decades, as a result of experience and sharing the knowledge from those experiences, companies have silently and collectively been crafting a concept of business ethics that is considerably broader than good, old-fashioned beliefs about right and wrong. As Laura Nash noted in the title of her book on business ethics, *Good Intentions Aside* (1993), good intentions on the part of our business leaders are no longer enough. As citizens, employees, managers, customers, suppliers, and consumers, we also demand that companies operate out of a clearly articulated set of values and that their ethical and compassionate reach extends not only to everyone within the company walls but also to those outside it as well. In addition, there are just plain legal requirements and guidelines to which we all, individuals and companies alike, must adhere. In addition to legal compliance and individual virtue, we clamor for clearly articulated concepts of what companies stand for and organizations that are socially responsible as well—a tall order.

Each of us comes to an organization, whether it be a two or three person entrepreneurial start-up operation or a Fortune 50 company, with our own set of personal values. These are our assumptions about what's fair, what's equitable, and what's right and wrong. These assumptions are deeply colored and influenced by whom we grew up with, what our experiences have been, how we have been rewarded, how we personally have succeeded in our culture, and what religious or nonreligious influences we were exposed to. These values and our sets of assumptions about how we see the world frequently are so deeply embedded that we do not talk about them unless we are asked to focus specifically on them, to make the implicit explicit. Only when we encounter a situation that flies in the face of our assumptions do we stop to question the assumptions or put a stake in the ground around our own beliefs, step back, and name the beliefs for what they are.

Individuals often make decisions that are driven by a personal core of values. More and more companies are beginning to define collective values within the organization as an attempt to communicate to employees, customers, and shareholders what they stand for, wish to be known for, or are striving to become. One good working definition of corporate values is "operational qualities used by organizations to maintain or enhance performance" (Harmon 1996).

The General Electric Company articulated a set of nine values a few years ago around which it makes its strategic decisions for the company as a whole and for individual businesses, and from which emerges all leadership development training. Storage Technology, the global data-tape retrieval system organization based in Louisville, Colorado, identified a set of company values as it emerged from bankruptcy in 1987. McGladry and Pullen, a large U.S. middle market accounting firm based in Cedar Rapids, Iowa, has used its corporate values as a checklist for moving through strategic changes and new directions for the company during the last 3 years.

Organizations use the process of developing core values as a means for getting their arms around the "softer" side of managing and working in organizations today. Developing clear statements on organizational values has become a means of helping an organization measure performance against those values. The process by which corporate values are defined takes different forms. In some cases, values are formulated at the top and handed down by fiat. Some corporate values are clearly formulated and articulated through an organizational process of input, communication, dialogue, and debate. Other corporate values are just simply lived out through policy or practice in the day-to-day world of doing business. Attitudes about what is expected of the individual in terms of work hours, the priority of the company in employees' lives, homelife-worklife balance, and downsizing and outsourcing may not be formulated as corporate values, but the intent is clear and the effect is clearly experienced. Regardless of how they are formulated, corporate values have become targets for ethical judgments by both employees and outside observers.

In other references to and conversations about business and ethics, we often refer to attitudes and behaviors under the label of corporate responsibility or social responsibility. These are the issues that cause one to ask the following:

- What is the responsibility of organizations to address the larger social issues of our time, issues businesses themselves are responsible for causing or making worse, such as environmental degradation or unemployment, or issues that simply exist in our society and affect the individuals in it?
- What policies do organizations institute to deal with job insecurity and its effect on community life, the widening gap between the haves and the havenots, environmental recklessness, or the economic well-being of minorities and other oppressed classes?

Our national biography has several sad chapters that highlight failures to respond to these crises when we have generated them—the arrogant disregard of public safety accompanied by corporate deception exemplified by the wanton chemical polluting of upper New York State's Love Canal; the lack of due diligence around cultural issues in the workplace as exemplified by the Union Carbide disaster in Bhopal, India; the dismissive attitude and neglect of corporate responsibility in the clean-up of the *Exxon Valdez* oil disaster. These highly visible incidents have become cultural shorthand for unethical business practices by U.S. companies.

THE THREE LEVELS OF DIALOGUE AND ENGAGEMENT ON BUSINESS AND ETHICS

In addition to the different types of values associated with application of ethics in the business environment—individual values, corporate values, and social responsibility—there are three ways those values are articulated in organizational life.

Figure 1.3 The Levels of Corporate Ethics Codes and Policies

Official Corporate Policy

U.S. organizations, including the U.S. government itself, have identified clear expectations about ethical business practices when doing business with other countries. The Foreign Corrupt Practices Act (FCPA), passed in 1977, forbids employees at companies working outside the U.S. from accepting bribes from other business or political groups and authorizes heavy fines and imprisonment for violation. Especially in recent years, as a result of the Sentencing Guidelines of 1991, which radically reduces penalties for organizations in violation of the law, organizations have gone to great lengths to define and publish their own guidelines regarding ethical practices. These guidelines and policies are communicated through various modes, such as training sessions, annual reports, and corporate gatherings, among others.

The General Electric Integrity Program is an example of a clearly defined policy on ethical behavior, although like most ethics codes, it is primarily weighted on the issues of compliance with U.S. laws (*Integrity: The Spirit and the Letter of Our Commitment,* General Electric internal publication, 1993). The program is highly visible throughout the organization in written documents as well as organizational culture and mindset and covers a typical array of situations for which it provides straightforward legal counsel. Situations covered under this legal guidance include the following:

Ethical business practice

Following international trade controls

Prohibitions on business with South Africa

Supplier relations

Working with government agencies

Complying with antitrust laws

Equal employment opportunity

Health, safety, and environmental protection

Participation in hazardous business

Financial controls and records

Avoiding conflicts of interest

Insider trading and stock tipping

Half day "Integrity Training" sessions have been held throughout every business division of the company worldwide. Every management class at its leadership development institute hears a talk by the chief legal counsel on potential ethical violations.

Honeywell Corporation considers its corporate ethics code the means to "fill the gaps in the law left open to interpretation," and communicates them worldwide as the Honeywell Principles. Whirlpool's ethics statement reads as follows:

> No employee of this company will ever be called upon to do anything in the line of duty that is morally, ethically, or legally wrong. Furthermore, if in the operation of this complex enterprise, an employee should come upon circumstances of which he or she cannot be personally proud, it should be that person's duty to bring it to the attention of top management if unable to correct the matter in any other way.

The communication of these highly visible policies is intended to inform and reassure shareholders, employees, and the world economic markets at large that by thinking through these issues of ethics and articulating standards for them regardless of how broad or generic, the organization has recognized an obligation to due diligence in this important aspect. Employees can breathe a sigh of relief that they will not be expected to engage in behaviors or decisions personally repugnant to them.

These visible, often well-crafted, and glossily presented public statements are what are usually referred to when companies speak about their ethical standards and practices. Particularly with managers from General Electric, a company with which I have consulted, references to "our Integrity Program" come up often in conversation. These corporate statements presumably define expectations for the conduct of personal behavior within the fulfillment of the duties of manager. But there is compelling evidence that statements of ethical practice—for all the hours and effort that go into them—are in many cases little more than window dressing and that rather than offering useful clarification, such statements set up painfully difficult dilemmas.

In January 1998, the results of a survey about ethics policies and codes at Fortune 1000 companies, conducted jointly by the business schools from Penn State University and the University of Delaware, concluded that these codes and policies may be primarily symbolic. Of 254 firms responding to the survey, 98 percent claimed to address ethics in a formal document, but only 51 percent required an annual statement of compliance from employees. "One surprise we had," said Gary Weaver from the University of Delaware, "was that while 137 of the firms reported having a single officer responsible for ethics, more than half of them actually spend not more than 10 percent of their time in ethics-related activities." Only 19 firms reported having a full-time ethics officer. Only 10 percent said they frequently survey external stakeholders about the firm's ethics (*Business Ethics* March/April 1998).

Does this mean that the efforts that go into developing and communicating ethics codes and policies are a sham, a waste of time? Not necessarily. The process of articulating corporate values and how companies want to engage with each other and with society as a whole is valuable in that it forces a group of leaders to engage in thinking and dialogue about difficult issues. What *is* problematic is that most organizations go no farther than the glossy brochure, the 1-hour training program, the ethics officer who works on ethics issues 10 percent of the time. Chapter 6 describes leaders who do more with their ethical intentions. In those firms we see a pattern of best practices emerging. Having organizational statements of ethical codes is an essential and imperative first step. But it is only the first step, as we see in Chapter 6.

The Effect of Corporate Policies on Day-to-Day Business Operations

Regardless of how clearly ethical policies, practices, and standards are developed and communicated within the internal boundaries of the corporation, when an individual manager is in the throes of running a business day to day in another culture, situations constantly arise that are difficult to correlate with an item in an ethics code. Managers frequently cite problems in getting materials, parts, and other deliverables through customs, motivating a local labor force, enforcing satisfactory standards in factory floor operations, and attending to human resource issues. Conflict between the corporate ethics policy and the day-

Figure 1.4 The Effect of Corporate Policies on Day-to-Day Business

to-day necessities of running the business is illustrated by the manager of a large Russian-American joint venture. Knowing that the company's policy, as well as the FCPA, strictly prohibits bribery, I asked how they were doing in getting their engine parts cleared through customs. The answer was as follows:

> We use shippers—companies like DHL, Fedex, Airborne Express— that move packages, and they encounter inordinate delays unless they have made some accommodation. We never know that directly, but that's what we hear "on the street"—that's if you haven't made some kind of arrangement, that's why you're running into big delays in customs. But we don't know directly, we hear that indi- rectly. The large factories we deal with all generally maintain small

offices in Moscow. A lot of offices have been approached by the organized thugs for protection money. They share that with us. I don't know [if they are approached but refuse to engage in the bribery or if they pay it] what they do. We do know they've been approached.

Another manager from another large joint venture said matter of factly "We have to pay big bucks to get things out of customs. . . . They know that foreigners have the money, so we have to pay. They can demand payment." At a General Electric meeting involving Russian and U.S., the general manager responsible for all business activities and market development in Moscow and the Commonwealth of Independent States, responded to a salesperson's lament that "other corporations are willing to pay bribes" with an emphatic, "GE will not do that. We have to be prepared to walk away from any deal if that is part of the deal."

The law does not prohibit all kinds of bribes, however. It does not, for example, prohibit payments made to managers of private companies, nor does it rule out modest "facilitating" payments. It is interesting to note, though, that managers do not make this distinction when talking about cross-cultural ethics.

One manager I've worked with argues that bribery is always categorically wrong and often claims, "I've never paid one penny!" Critics of FCPA argue that it poses a disadvantage for U.S. firms in competition with foreign companies, because many countries, including other western countries, do not have such laws. However, according to several studies, statistical evidence suggests that U.S. firms *have not* lost market share in countries or regions where the FCPA has changed U.S. practices (Green 1994). Even though it does not require that all payments be outlawed, the law does provide a credible and consistent way for honest managers to communicate their unwillingness to play by rules that compromise their values.

One senior executive I know is an "intrapreneur" from a very large insurance conglomerate. Even though he works for a large corporation, he has been given the authority and freedom to run a separate joint venture that involves lumbering in Asia. He has encountered a succession of obstacles in moving lumber across the country and then out to other countries and is frequently approached for bribes and payoffs for transportation. "I'm representing a large American company and we cannot engage in behavior perceived as unethical, such as bribery. We were having difficulty with customs inspectors with our trains. So instead of leaving our lumber open to pilfering because we weren't paying the bribes, I locked myself in the train along with a guard in order to get our goods through."

The Individual Manager

When managers work globally, whether they are living permanently overseas as expatriates, or, more often, as global managers with virtual offices and teams in several if not dozens of countries,

Figure 1.5 Effect of Corporate Policies on the Individual Manager

the engagement in ethical decision making is not only on the level of the company operations but also on the individual and personal level in hundreds of everyday encounters. Individuals are forced to find ways to make sense out of the intersection of their personal values and the culture they are experiencing. As one middle-aged manager running a U.S. operation in Russia commented:

> Americans deal with it [corruption] on a personal level. There's always fear. When Americans get here they get a shipment [of their personal goods], which has to go through customs. Guess who controls customs? Anything that involves getting permission, like buying a car, requires you to pay big bucks. Every time you want any kind of license or permission to use your car, to do this or do that— permission to do anything—you have to pay somebody money. These aren't things that you can run to your boss about every time you have a question or need an answer. You just have to figure it out on your own and go on. It happens a hundred times a day.

INTEGRATING CORPORATE POLICIES, BUSINESS PRACTICES, AND PERSONAL VALUES

In this gap between the public, corporate ethical stand and good intentions of companies and the mechanics of day-to-day operations, managers become individual moral navigators, simultaneously conducting interpretations, implementations, and audits on their company's policies and their own values. Here they must constantly calibrate their behaviors and actions against their own personal values and cultural guidelines. Knowing the clearly stated public guidelines helps the individuals at their launch point for ethical decision making. It often is left to the individual, however, to make sense of the guidelines in a way that allows them to make a profit and make it ethically. It is difficult work. It can be grueling, emotional work.

WHY ANOTHER BOOK ON BUSINESS ETHICS

There is no shortage of books on business ethics these days. Popular trade books focus on the entire gamut of business ethics realms, from ethical strategies and implications for leaders to

16

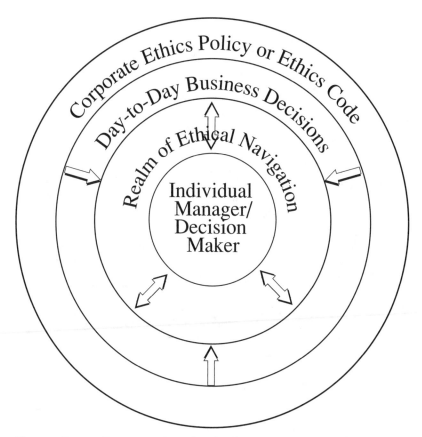

Figure 1.6 The manager and individual employee are constantly making organizational and personal decisions, always within the context of what the organization has communicated as expectations of ethical behavior and what the business requires to make a profit.

the effect of corporate decisions on the personal lives and worlds of employees to the issues of social responsibility. Best practices for developing core values and managing for responsibility are beginning to surface and provide a wealth of helpful stories and information.

Many of the books on business ethics are presented as case study books to be used with MBA courses in management or business ethics. They present ethical dilemmas through the time-honored tradition of case studies. They frequently use the same internationally known high-profile cases mentioned earlier

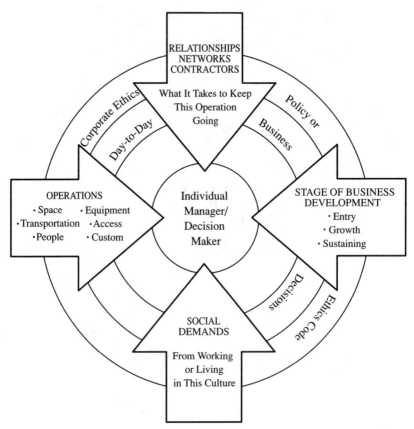

Figure 1.7 Constellation of Ethical Decisions and Demands on Manager in Cross-Cultural Business Interactions

(Love Canal, Exxon Valdez, Union Carbide and Bhopal). There is usually some passing nod to the fact that understanding business ethics in a cross-cultural context is important, complex, and needs further study. Maybe there is a short chapter at the end of the book or the addition of a few paragraphs onto another chapter acknowledging the difficulties of applying ethical practices in other cultures. There is some mention of the FCPA, a footnoted reference to the 1991 Sentencing Guidelines, or an entertaining list of cultural dos and taboos.

So far, however, no one has explored these dilemmas from the perspective of individual U.S. managers, specifically those working in a cross-cultural and global environment, using the lens of their own personal values intersecting corporate policy and highlighted through their own words, stories, and dilemmas. That's what we do here. These managers are the intermediaries faced with the necessity of calibrating the balance among their own personal and cultural values, the policies of the organization, and the day-to-day necessities of making a profit and making it ethically. *Navigating Cross-Cultural Ethics* is a look at how global managers actually navigate the translation of organizational ethics policies into their daily business decisions and personal values. It is also the first book to provide recommendations for helping managers deal with the inevitable dilemmas that result from this complex formula. It is a personal look into the lives of individual managers in their roles as "moral navigators"of the corporation.

Chapter 2 explores the urgent need for understanding business and ethics in global companies and why it has so quickly become an urgent corporate issue. This chapter explains why finding ways to navigate effectively in these waters is no longer a nice-to-do but an essential must-do.

Chapter 3 explores in depth a particular cross-cultural business relationship between Russians and Americans. It highlights the implicit assumptions that are played out but seldom articulated or understood in day-to-day business interactions.

Chapter 4 provides a framework for creating an ethical map that helps you understand how to determine what issues are really in play in cross-cultural transactions and why some cause more difficulty for us as U.S. managers than others. The different aspects of the map are highlighted by the stories of managers who actually struggle with those issues.

Chapter 5 helps you understand your choices as an individual or an organization in journeying with the ethical map. It presents stories about managers who are navigating in different arenas of the map and how they can move from one area of the ethical map to another.

Chapter 6 takes a close look at what leaders can do to build ethical competence in their organizations. They share their stories, their wisdom, and the best practices around ethical leadership that are beginning to emerge.

Listening to the conversation between my friend Andrei and the Americans launched me on an exploration to find some clarity and new perspectives about what actually goes on during business interactions in global organizations. Where do the misunderstandings, accusations, and mistrust originate? Where are the possibilities for building common ground, new ground, or simply clearer ground? How does the individual manager make sense of conflicting messages and expectations? The stories in the following pages are the stories of the voyagers themselves. I add my own stories as simply another voyager in these ill-explored waters.

Just like the voyages of the early explorers, the journey of navigating through this deeply complex and rich new territory, for those willing to undertake it, can yield unexpected riches, new knowledge, and certainly new personal insights. What we do not know we fear. The maps of the early explorers were richly detailed in their drawings of the known universe. The lands were surrounded by seas and oceans, bordered on all sides with the warning: DRAGONS BE HERE. Join this journey and discover where the dragons live—in yourself as a manager, in your organization's practices and policies, and in the unexplored global waters of business and ethics.

> Oh, lay down your burden
> Oh, lay it all down
> Pass the glass between you, drink it up
> Light the light before you
> Come through the door
> The dragon doesn't live here anymore.

> *Words by Marilyn Redfield*
> *Performed by Paul Winter Consort*

Chapter 2

The Rising Storm of Business Ethics in Global Organizations

"In organizations, we are at the edge of this new world of relationships hoping the new charts are true still fearing if we follow them, that we will fall off into nothing."

... MARGARET WHEATLEY, 1992

"Having a well stamped passport isn't enough to make an executive a global player."

... RICHARD M. PERRY, PRESIDENT, KORN-FERRY

Why does the topic of business and ethics come up frequently in conversations in the hallways and cafeterias of global companies these days? Why do accounts of personal dilemmas work their way into the conversations of every corporate classroom where participants are exploring the meaning of leadership in today's organizations? What has been changing in the structure of organizations that has resulted in an increasing sense of urgency and disease in this area of ethics, values, and personal behavior in organizations?

In this chapter, we explore why there is a growing urgency to be able to understand and operate a business ethically in global companies. In every organization in which I work conversations about moral conflicts, questionable practices, and questionable behavior are more common than ever before. The reason for this is that in companies in the United States and around the world there is a new and complex intersection of important events, as follows:

1. The economic fundamentals of the globe are changing
2. More and more business is conducted in third world countries and developing nations
3. More individuals throughout the organization interact in a global capacity

We operate out of a predominantly, if not exclusively, western ethical perspective. We have long operated in the comfort zone in which the meaning of contracts is inherently understood, honored, and the basis for all business transactions. Along with the inherent belief in the value of contracts has been the equally strong belief in the role of personal accountability in carrying out those contracts. A fundamental shift in our economic foundation has directly affected the assumptions that make up our ethical foundations.

FUNDAMENTAL GLOBAL ECONOMIC CHANGE

Lester Thurow, in a speech to the International Strategic Management Conference (1996) in Atlanta, Georgia, described these fundamental economic shifts as being like the tectonic plates of the earth, those massive geologic structures that form the earth's surfaces and hold up life as we know it on the planet. When those geologic plates shift out of their existing positions, everything else must shift along with them, causing ruptures on the surface and a reordering of all that currently exists. When these ruptures occur in the earth's crust, we label them *earthquakes*. However, long before the earth actually erupts in a real and visible way, the plates underneath the earth have begun shifting without notice on the surface. These geologic plates lie far below the surface and can shift slowly and imperceptibly over tens and hundreds of years before anyone notices anything on the surface. The trends start to occur over a period of time, but it is not until there is a fundamental shifting of these plates that we feel the effect on land. That is what is happening in our society and in organizations today. Even though changes have started below the level of what we perceive in everyday life, as an organizational consultant I have begun to feel the tremors in many companies with which I work.

ORGANIZATIONAL IMPLICATIONS OF FUNDAMENTAL GLOBAL CHANGE

Fundamental changes in economic pressures are having a direct effect on what has been happening in countries around us and have had a significant effect on the dynamics of business and ethics in global companies. We need to explore three key developments in U.S. business to understand how and why this increase in tension has occurred—globalization, downsizing and outsourcing, and decentralization of decision making.

Globalization

Globalization—the fundamental change in how we do business—is the first key development and significantly affects the other key changes. Globalization is affecting our awareness of business and ethics in global companies, simply because more business is being conducted by U.S. companies globally.

U.S. businesses are doing business in more markets than ever before. March 1998 U.S. Import and Export statistics from the U.S. Department of Commerce indicated that there were 9 percent and 10 percent increases respectively, between 1996 and 1997 figures alone. These figures, of course, do not reflect the billions of dollars in goods and services generated internally by U.S. companies and U.S. joint ventures within the borders of other countries. At the same time that U.S. companies are doing more business in more new markets than ever before, they are accomplishing it at increasing speed. More U.S. companies are doing business abroad through alliances, joint ventures, and collaborations and in U.S.-owned production facilities. Our business world is calibrated at a faster pace, and the sheer growth in numbers of the companies making these relatively swift changes is affecting globalization. More day-to-day transactions with employees, customers, suppliers, and partners are being conducted in countries and cultures outside the U.S. What follows are examples of companies finding new ways to survive and thrive in the new global markets.

TEXAS INSTRUMENTS: SHARING INFORMATION, BUILDING GLOBAL PARTNERSHIPS

Back in the mid1980s, Texas Instruments was almost forced out of the market for dynamic Random Access Memory chips (DRAMs) by Asian rivals. Its market share declined from 11 percent to 5 percent. Instead of folding up and conceding that market to its rivals, as many U.S. chip makers did, Texas Instruments developed and executed a radical strategy. In 1987, the company began to share information about its research on the next generation of DRAMs with its biggest competitor, Hitachi, Ltd. Soon the dialogue was expanded to NEC, AT&T, Intel, Sharp, and a consortium of IBM, Toshiba, and Siemens. Texas Instruments followed this experiment with a series of joint ventures to build plants with Italy, Taiwanese personal computer maker Acer, Japan's Kobe Steel, and a consortium in Singapore that included Hewlett-Packard, Canon, and the Singapore government. Today a telecommunication chip "made" by Texas Instruments is the product of engineering from the Erickson Telephone Company in Sweden. Designed in Nice with Texas Instruments software tools developed in Houston, it is produced in Japan and Dallas, tested in Taiwan, and wired into Erickson linecards that monitor phone systems in Sweden, the United States, Mexico, and Australia. Today 65 percent of the company's chip sales are outside the United States. On the sales and marketing side of the business, worldwide teams of product specialists, including executives and factory workers, go from country to country to troubleshoot and are working hard to eliminate geographic silos (*Business Week* August 7, 1995).

MOBIL CORPORATION: BREAKING DOWN THE PIECES

Early in 1996, Mobil Corporation made a decision to form 11 business units out of its traditional hierarchy of three global divisions. Mobil's business units are complete microorganizations of Mobil, and each can fully deal with all customer needs, from both the product aspect and the marketing and refining aspect. As one former Mobil executive put it, "Before, if you wanted to do anything in eastern Europe you had to go through Mobil in Germany and Mobil in London, now that's all gone. The people in eastern Europe can deal with people directly in Fairfax" (*World Perspective* September/October 1996). Mobil's CEO, Lucio Noto, emphasizes that the thrust of the new organization isn't about cost reduction but about expanding Mobil's business globally, allowing their newest markets, Latin America and the former Soviet Union, to focus on growth and performance. In the meantime, Mobil's revenues have increased from 54 billion in 1985 to 75 billion today, while the number of its employees has plunged from 75,000 to 50,000.

Down(Sizing) and Out(Sourcing) in U.S. Business: The Fundamental Restructuring of Organizations to Meet New Global Demands

To function with speed and flexibility in the new marketplace, many companies have taken the route of streamlining their workforces. This affects ethical issues in global companies directly because fewer people are doing more jobs, and therefore simply more people are involved in the global aspects of their business.

A companion to increasing globalization and a second tectonic force that affects the need to deal with business ethics more intentionally, is the ongoing trend to decrease the size of the workforce in organizations through either downsizing or outsourcing. The reasoning seems to be if we can make it or buy it for less somewhere else and make us look better to our stockholders because of reduced operational overhead, that's all that's required by us to justify doing it.

Look at the recent trend. According to Challenger and Gray's 1996 survey of company layoffs, downsizing during the last few years peaked in 1993, when approximately 220,000 persons were laid off, fell off during the next few years, and then hit almost 200,000 persons in 1996 (*Business Week* May 20, 1996). Like most major shifts in today's organizations, there is no simple rationale or point of view about the reason for or wisdom of these cuts. Some even argue the actual numbers, stating that these figures do not accurately reflect the total intricacies of the economy. Regardless of one's political, sociologic, or organizational opinion of the layoffs, it is clear to anyone working in today's corporations that more work is being done by fewer people. All you have to do is sit in any meeting in any company with a team of employees. Everywhere I go in organizations I hear the following:

"I've got too much on my plate already."

"I'm wearing at least two hats here."

"Now I'm doing my old job and the jobs of the three people who were just let go as well."

"I'm snowed under."

"I'm working 60 hours a week just to keep up."

"I come in extra early in the morning just to have some quiet time and time to read my E-mail."

My personal favorite, overheard in the cafeteria line of a major corporation: "I'm exhausted. I've worked the last two weekends in a row on our work-life balance program."

GENERAL ELECTRIC WORK-OUT: ELIMINATING JOBS BUT NOT WORK

In the mid1980s, General Electric Company downsized its world-wide workforce by more than 100,000 employees. In the late 1980s, Jack Welch commented that, "The people have gone away but the work hasn't." In response to this awareness, he launched the most ambitious work elimination process undertaken in corporate America at that time, a culture change and improvement process known as Work-Out™. Perhaps the most famous organizational intervention of the 1990s (Tichy and Sherman 1993; Slater 1994; Ashkenas et al. 1995), Work-Out™ launched hundreds of employee dialogue and work improvement sessions throughout the company. Groups of people who worked together spent 2 to 3 days intensely focusing on how they did their work, from clerical systems and processes, ordering, manufacturing, invoicing, new product introductions, customer service, and pricing. One thing was clear throughout all the sessions. Fewer people were doing more work. Even when non–value-added work was recognized and eliminated, new, more-value-added processes were there to take their place. Decisionmaking was pushed down to its lowest level of contact in the organization. Employees tried to figure out how to work smarter at the same time that they were working harder and longer.

STORAGE TECHNOLOGY CORPORATION: DOWNSIZING FOR RESTRUCTURING

Emerging from Chapter 11 bankruptcy in 1987, Storage Technology Corporation, a manufacturer of large-frame magnetic tape storage components, based in Louisville, Colorado, with world-wide markets, still had a tough road ahead. From the late 1980s through the mid1990s, it went through a series of layoffs to downsize the newly emerged company into a leaner organization. Early in 1996, it launched an organizational effort to lead change around five strategic initiatives of the company. Storage Technology launched a series of WorkSmart sessions similar in design to

General Electric's Work-Out™ and designed with the intention to alleviate the crushing blow of day-to-day work resulting from the decline in the workforce. Managers such as human resource executives who already held full-time-plus responsible senior positions were asked to take on another full-time assignment such as management of a major change leadership process, providing leadership for all systemic change efforts on a corporationwide basis. Business leaders and vice presidents were required to take on management of multimillion dollar marketing integration plans and processes. Employees on the manufacturing floor put in many additional hours on weekends and holidays.

IT'S NOT JUST THE ONES WHO GO

Corporate downsizing and restructuring definitely affect people who leave a company. They also have an enormous and powerful effect on the people who stay, the ones who assume the extra workload and who struggle to make sense of and be productive in the new corporate structure.

One of the human resource consultants this has affected works for a large global company. Her primary client base is the financial operations center of 600 people. After several years of downsizing at the company, her job was radically restructured from compensation manager to "internal organizational development consultant." Typical of such job realignments, she and her colleagues were given no training or preparation before jumping into their new roles. She says:

> The thing that is most different in terms of the last mass reorganization, is that there's a full realization that the contract at work is different. It has the most impact in terms of how people view their jobs and the loyalty they feel and express to this company. We've had so many layoffs that people fully comprehend there is no job security. We're moving towards career resiliency, which means that employees are expected to take more responsibility for their work lives and for their career development. The emphasis is on being employable but not necessarily staying with this company. We've opened Career Resource Centers which are

manned by outside career consultants. They use the Internet and they're finding people jobs outside of the organization. And yet management is surprised that people are leaving. Not just the downsized and outplaced people, but also the people in the company that haven't been asked to leave and now have some new skills and some new confidence. The emphasis is that there's not so much a commitment to the company or to the long term but to the actual job itself and how you can keep yourself afloat.

In a recent update on our previous conversation about life in the newly downsized organization, the same human resources consultant acknowledged that she is now heading a special task force for employee retention because so many people chose to leave the company. In addition, because it has completely revamped all its internal systems, the company needs employee talent who can deal effectively with the new systems and maintain the remaining ones. "We broke the contract, people took us seriously, and now we're up the creek," the human resources consultant stated ruefully.

Stanley J. Schrager, a Senior Vice-President of the Chase Manhattan Bank for 27 years, has seen the changes that have taken place, not only in the banking industry but also in Chase Manhattan Bank in particular. The recent merger with Chemical Bank resulted in many persons' being let go and jobs being shifted around.

Sitting in his office at 240 Park Avenue one brilliant fall day, Stan reflected:

The amount of stress that's around here is just enormous. People have to learn how to adjust to a new culture, new management structure, and new ways of doing business. Let me tell you a story about how the organization is responding to all of this stress as a result of the downsizing. There's a person who worked for me who not too long ago dropped dead of a heart attack at work. The immediate assumption by everyone in the organization who knew him, as well as those who only heard about the incident, was that it happened because he was working so hard. Because of all the restructuring, the merger and the downsizing, he had just been pushed to his limit in the most extreme and visible way possible.

When a company goes through a major downsizing and restructuring, the public results are always framed in terms of benefit to the shareholder, such as the increase in profits and the positive yields in productivity. All this downsizing and restructuring to compete more effectively in a global marketplace has contributed to difficult dynamics in the everyday life of managers and others at work. When viewed from inside the corporation or through the eyes of an outside consultant like me, the story you hear is quite different, quite painful, and quite personal:

1. People feel demoralized.
2. People feel they're just not valued.
3. There's anxiety about where the business itself is going.
4. There's confusion about who's in charge.
5. There's distrust and there's a lot of it.

"There's a lot of confusion about the systems that keep things in place, and not just the technical systems. Nothing works the way it used to. We've stripped out systems and people, and so many systems are specific to our company," says another human resources consultant. "Nothing's like it used to be. People say, 'I don't know where to go or who to turn to.' All this delayering—no one understands how decisions get made. What does empowerment mean anyway? How does the work get done? There's no way we can ever get all the work done. We just simply don't do some of it."

The Decentralization of Decision Making

In parallel to the restructuring and downsizing of organizations in the 1990s, the "empowerment movement" emerged swiftly and strongly in many companies. Just in case we want to pat ourselves on the back for implementing such a powerful structural work and organization tool, the following is evidence that empowerment (or pushing decision making down to the lowest level in the organization that can make the decision) is a concept that's been around for a while. Here are some words from what must be one of the earliest organizational observers:

"The way that you are managing is not good. The job before you is too hard and both you and the people with you will suffer if you try to do it alone. You must provide direction but the people must make decisions about things that they know the most about."

. . . JETHRO TO MOSES, EXODUS 18:17–22

One of the most important things about the increasing decentralization of decision making in organizations is that it has meant the uncoupling of global contact from strict, centralized, departmental control. This control has been loosened to include individual business units with many more managers, employees, customers, and suppliers who actually touch the part of the business transacted in other parts of the world.

I have taught at General Electric's Leadership Development Institute, informally known as Crotonville, for almost a decade. One of the courses I have taught over the years is called the *New Manager Development Course*. This intensive week-long residential program of business and leadership exercises and content is for managers who are new to the manager function, are in positions to lead work teams, or are young General Electric employees who are now in managerial or team leader functions. Whether it is people involved in direct sales or people involved in running the operations on a manufacturing floor, managers are simply having more contact with their counterparts around the world. General Electric Lighting production managers and team leaders now deal directly with their counterparts at General Electric Tungsram, in Hungary, and other affiliates in India and the United Kingdom. Individual business units now have geographic responsibility for all of the sales, marketing, vendor, and customer relationships that take place in those countries.

Teaching, talking, and working with hundreds of these managers over the past decade has been a living example of what Peter Vaill, management professor, consultant, and author, refers to when he talks about "whitewater"management. Whitewater is Vaill's metaphor for the constantly churning economic, political, and business environment in which companies must operate today. Vaill (1989) also sees the direct effects of whitewater and the increasing decentralization of business operations:

> More decentralization also creates more "Whitewater" because it substantially increases the number of points in a complex system where managers are empowered to take major initiatives without having to go through a lengthy approval process up the line. The net effect is that change is being initiated from many points in the organizational network, not just from the top. A growing feeling of loss of meaning derives from several sources. Whitewater events often contain a clash of logics and priorities as asserted by various stakeholder groups, such as customers, supplier, owners, competitors, and employees.

If we are feeling this loss of meaning from the clash of logics and priorities from working in our own companies in our own culture, imagine the repercussions of expanding that experience to include other companies in other cultures. The feelings of loss of meaning can only ripple out even farther.

The transition from thoroughly understanding what you are about, what your company is about and what the boundaries and parameters of operating your business are about to navigating the relativism of making sense of all of these in other cultures in context is agonizing. When we made business decisions and engaged in interpersonal relationships solely from the safe and familiar harbor of our own personal and cultural values, we could move ahead with some sense of confidence. According to Vaill (1989):

> Our own growth, our ever increasing sophistication and knowledge of the cultures and value systems may also be contributing to our feelings of uncertainty and confusion. Relativism may be a more practical and defensible philosophy than absolutism, but at the personal level the transition from one to the other can be agonizing. Who is right in the various debates that are sweeping through societal and organizational life? When we didn't know this . . . it was a lot simpler.

When perestroika occurred in Russia along with the literal uncoupling of the republics from the state of Russia, a period of confusion and chaos was launched from which there are many repercussions today. Whereas previously the Soviet Union had been powerfully managed from a central state and a central dynamic force, perestroika shifted that power to the individual Russian states. Whereas once a manager negotiating sales in Russia dealt with the central office of Aeroflot in Moscow, he or she later had to deal with Aeroflot in several Russian states. Now shifting once again from individual state control to private enterprise, that same manager must deal with innumerable private companies in several states simultaneously, all without the benefit of longstanding, carefully nurtured personal and business relationships (Tourevski and Morgan 1993). Business dealings and knowing whom to deal with in Russia had been quite clear, if not simple, when one was trying to orchestrate deals for airplane or locomotive engines. The clarity disappeared overnight, and transactions suddenly had to be worked through many states separately. Clarity has receded even further into memory with the emergence of private enterprises within the many states.

U.S. companies have engaged in a parallel process at home and in their worldwide operations by decentralizing and decoupling their international departments. Gone are the days of the International Department that dealt exclusively with contacts outside the United States. Many companies have shifted to a global marketing format in which each line of business deals directly with whomever it has to deal wherever it wants to deal. Having direct contact with global partners has meant an immediate effect on managers at all levels who are now at the center of those contacts.

RESULTS

Alone, each of these forces affects the current shift around business and ethics. Combined, they have a powerful effect. So what have been the results of effects of globalization and the changes in the global economy, restructuring and downsizing, and decentralization of decision making on ethical decision making in the global company? Responsibility and accountability for ethical decision making and ethical behavior have been moved down in the organization along with all other kinds of decision making, simply because more people are touching the decisions.

One of the reasons that this issue of business and ethics has become more visible is that the organizational and individual perceptions of ethics as a "corporate public relations issue" has changed dramatically. Ethical issues no longer are incidents on a grand scale of high visibility that can be handled by the corporate communications department. There has been a shift, out of survival and necessity, to view ethical issues as issues of individual accountability, the intersection of organizational and personal values. There is clearly an awareness of the individual decision making required by more employees in more cultural situations around more transactions. No longer can we point to and read about high-profile company-wide ethical "problems," such as the Union Carbide Bhopal incident, the *Exxon Valdez* incident, and the Nestle "problem" with infant formula in Africa. As more people experience this personal aspect of individual decision making and responsibility in organizations, they begin to see that these ethical decisions are made every day on a hundred different levels.

The second result is that there has been an organizational response to this change in how business is accomplished globally. Many companies now have developed codes of conduct. Partially in response to comply with the 1991 Sentencing Guidelines, which soften the penalties meted out if a company is convicted of an ethical violation, many companies have developed these codes of ethics. An extensive survey by the Ethics Resource Center in Washington, D.C. (Goodall 1994) indicated that 60 percent of their respondents reported they had a code of conduct. Another study by The Conference Board showed the number to be as high as 84 percent in U.S. companies. Other companies, however, are making an honest attempt to provide some guidance and some support to all employees and their organizations as they deal with ever increasingly global and more complex decision making in running the business.

We have begun to accept that we are living in a world of swiftly changing economies that affect where companies are doing business and with whom. The pace of the change is no less exhausting than when it began to accelerate dramatically a decade ago, but the inevitability of it is becoming more familiar. We are a world economy that is expanding in ever growing concentric circles, each ripple having an effect on everything around us. At the same time, the rapidly growing emerging markets are generating concentric circles of commercial force of their own. The waves are meeting and crashing upon each other.

INCREASING GLOBALIZATION, INCREASING CHAOS

Peter Vail popularized the term *permanent whitewater* as a metaphor for what life today feels like in the chronically unsettled environment of organizations. The image is a corporate kayaker suited up and helmeted, paddle in hand, setting out on the rushing river of organizational life. With skill and precision the paddler maneuvers through the rough waters, narrowly avoiding protruding boulders, attacking the rapids, turning at just the right moments. Exhausted, the manager scans the immediate horizon to see where the water breaks through a place of calm where she can anticipate a chance to regroup, rest. But there is no smooth water ahead—only more rapids, new turns, more rocks. The increase of businesses into the areas of global markets, global production, global sales, and global strategies thrusts the manager of today's organization into a river of whitewater that pulses with nonstop change.

These changes have been more than metaphorical. In some cases they are concrete, happening right before our eyes. A few times in our history as a planet, we have had the experience of a single worldwide event that changed the world overnight as we, like a global family staying up late to not miss this amazing show, collectively watched on television. The fall of communism not only was a riveting piece of global drama, but also fundamentally changed the world and its organizations along with it. It was a prime example of what Lester Thurow (1996) referred to as changes in fundamental economic processes.

The fall of communism opened a new era of explosive expansion into global markets. Not only has a massive new market opened for the manufacture and sale of consumer goods, but also an unprecedented pool of brain power has become available to the world market at discounted prices. In addition to the unskilled labor traditionally leveraged in developing countries that today primarily constitutes the expansion of global markets, scientists, programmers, researchers, and other professionals have flooded the market to be snapped up by companies as employees or for contractual hire.

INCREASING GLOBALIZATION, INCREASING LABOR AND BRAIN POWER OPTIONS

Several years ago I worked with the corporate research and development business of a global firm. Until that time the research business had been run as corporate overhead, and funded centrally. The department had a captive customer base—the dozen or so profit centers and business segments of the organization required to use the services of the corporate research department. Requests from the business units for resources for research and development projects were in turn reprioritized by the corporate department. By its own admission, research and development had a tendency to work on what it pleased—whatever was of personal and professional interest to them as scientists and researchers. All of that changed overnight when an organizational restructuring turned the corporate research department into a stand-alone, zero-based budget profit center. Individual business units could now purchase research and development services from anywhere. Suddenly the research and development department found itself competing on projects with engineers from India and scientists from Hungary. The department was at a tremendous disadvantage in pricing its services because of its expensive overhead and high salaries. "Why should they [the business unit] pay more for using one of our $100,000+ scientists when it can get equal value from a scientist from eastern Europe for $800 a month," asked the leader of the business team assigned to tackle research and development's own internal structures and inefficiencies. "We have to compete with the rest of the world now," he concluded. The opening of vast new talent pools as a result of the fall of communism had a direct impact on the day-to-day operations of this corporate group and on the group's corporate clients. Globalization at work.

In the summer of 1991, my co-author, a Russian psychologist, and I turned in the first draft of a book manuscript originally titled *Cutting the Red Tape: How To Do Business in the Soviet Union.* Two weeks later the fall of communism across eastern Europe and the Baltic states brought the disintegration of the Soviet Union. Not once during the 18 months my co-author and I had spent working on the book did the thought ever cross our minds that there would be *no Soviet Union.* Several months later, after major rewrites, we submitted the second draft titled *Cutting the Red Tape: Doing Business with Russia and Her Republics* only to watch weeks later the devolution of the republics as they splintered off as independent states from mother Russia. Finally, in a desperate act of "getting it" we named the book *Cutting the Red Tape: How Western Companies Can Profit in the New Russia* (The Free Press, 1992). Shifting plates at work.

INCREASING GLOBALIZATION, INCREASING AWARENESS OF CHAOS

At the same time that managers are adjusting to new geography and different cultures, they are being required simultaneously to change, grow, and learn about

- new business products and services that are constantly evolving within their own business
- the business dynamics of new and changing world markets
- who they are as individuals and professionals in this changing context
- how to balance conflicting goals (more quality and more speed, faster product delivery and fewer people to do it, global capability and local presence)

Recently I was working in a corporation with a large group of managers who were at the peak of their frustration. They expressed anger and despair at the perceived lack of company strategy on the part of their leaders. "You say one thing one week and something else the next," they stated. "We start down one road and then a few months later it's changed." "There are things you're not telling us," accused another. "We've hardly settled down from one reorganization and another one is announced. Don't you people know what you want?" Finally, wearily, angrily one manager exclaimed, "There's got to be somebody at the top who knows what's happening here. It may be only one guy, but there's got to be at least one, and he's not telling!" This is a particularly clear and poignant cry for predictability, a publicly expressed longing for order and routine, for someone, anyone, to be in charge. We feel we are churning in the whitewater with no life vest and are about to lose our only paddle. We are standing on land that is widening with tremor after tremor. There is nowhere to hide.

When we add the extra dimension of navigating these constant changes in global waters the feeling of chaos is magnified. It's no wonder we feel "in over our heads," as Robert Kegan, the human development psychologist at Harvard University, describes the situation of life today. Kegan describes our day-to-day lives as a relentless barrage of paradoxes and contradictions—all truths—in which we must survive and thrive and upon which we must act our own lives (Kegan 1994).

With the advent of a global society, individuals and organizations have been cast into boats of all sizes and shapes to navigate the unknown waters. Like the explorers of the fifteenth century, we are both terrified and compelled to venture forth. Whom will we find? What riches await us? Where do the dragons lurk? The fear of the unknown also carries with it the allure of connection, of being a part of something even larger than ourselves—our present organizational configuration; our current definitions of what we call knowledge. What currently feel like disjointed eruptions based on whimsy, opportunity, greed, or perhaps impulse are new patterns finding their order, new plates repositioning, and new river courses rushing around the bend. Globalization is the twenty-first century adult version of the child's game of crack the whip. We rush headlong into the future of today, hurtling ourselves and those in our organizations along with us, forgetting that each of us in the chain no matter how far down feels the crack and responds to the impact. How that whip crack affects our ethical decision making in global companies is what we explore in the next chapters.

Chapter 3

Fate and Free Will: Meaning and Mirage

"There's no such thing as a weird human being. It's just that some people need a little more understanding than others."

... TOM ROBBINS

Chapter 2 examines the fundamental global economic changes that have triggered a cascading set of events that directly affect the day-to-day life in organizations. These changes—new and increasing numbers of global markets, downsizing and streamlining in organizations, and more people directly involved in day-to-day business transactions cross-culturally—have resulted in an increased need to understand and successfully navigate ethical issues in global companies.

In Chapter 3 we explore specific differences in ethical meaning using two specific cultures—Russian and American—and their business interactions in joint ventures. (I realize that when I use the label *American* it implies that only people from the United States are Americans. I realize this usage excludes the entire continent of South America as well as Mexico, Central America, and Canada. I apologize for the use of this term as a linguistic necessity for expediency.) To do this exploration, we have to go deeper than the usual "How To Do Business In. . . "

approach to cross-cultural business interactions. We'll take an in-depth look at the concepts of core values and the cultural and political assumptions that underlie the choices that lead to specific behavior at the deal table. Finally, we explore a new cross-cultural approach to ethics, which I have labeled *A Holographic Model for Global Business and Ethics*. This approach is more complex than the philosophic approaches used over the decades and taught in college philosophy and business courses. Yet it is more suitable and practical for the postmodern, global world in which we now transact business. This is an approach for managers who feel and indeed must operate, as Robert Kegan says "in over our heads."

THE CASE OF THE RUSSIAN-AMERICAN JOINT VENTURES

I have worked in Russia over a period of 10 years, first encountering the country when it was the Soviet Union, and trying to design and implement pre-perestroika citizen exchange programs. I slogged through interminable meetings with Directors of This and That in countless Ministries of This and That, between meetings touring the inevitable Museums of Everything Imaginable. Since then, I have worked with U.S. clients, their Russian and Ukrainian customers and suppliers, and a group of newly minted post-perestroika entrepreneurs. Remember my friend at the beginning of Chapter 1, Andrei Manokovsky, the director of the International Business School of Moscow? He was the Russian who was matter of factly trying to communicate the Culture of Corruption in the new business world in Russia and was met with anger and disagreement on the part of the Americans in that meeting. That perplexing interaction made me to want to explore a deeper understanding of how different cultures construct their meaning around this idea of business ethics, and why it so frequently becomes hopelessly tangled in webs of meaning and misunderstood meaning when business is conducted and the language becomes explicit. I had difficulty believing that Russians, or persons from any of the cultures with whom my business clients profess to have difficulty, choose to engage in ways that are constantly interpreted by westerners as deceitful and corrupt. Were they really that different? I decided to find out what kind of assumptions these managers made, both Russians and Americans, and what frames of reference and cultural touchstones they were using and carried in their own minds when they used the words *ethics* and *corruption*.

THE BUSINESS OF *BIZNEZ*

One of the main things I had to keep in mind when talking with Russians about business transactions was that Russians really have no word of their own for business. The word they used to represent the concept was the phonetic equivalent in their language of our English word. The word itself also carries enormous cultural baggage left over from the years of communism. The word *biznez* was an epithet used to connote the very essence of exploitation, corruption, and underhanded dealings that communists ascribed to capitalistic deal makers. The word and idea were what westerners identified as the corruption and illegalities against which they were railing, the behaviors they ascribed in one broad, inclusive cultural sweep to their Russian business partners. I wanted to anchor my understanding of how these concepts were used in actual behaviors by managers in business transactions—what they said and what they did. I wanted these concepts tied to the real world of day-to-day operations and business decisions made by real managers in real situations and not to those of sophomore college philosophy students or MBA students mulling over some hypothetical "What would you do if…"questionnaire or case study.

DUALITY VERSUS DUPLICITY

What emerged from talking with many managers about this topic of business and ethics was a clear distinction between Russians and Americans about what ethics and corruption mean in business interactions. Russians quite clearly make a distinction between the very ideas of business ethics and corruption. Because of their history with communism, corruption is viewed as behavior that is institutionally and hierarchically based and out of their control—as well as out of the control of their American partners. Business and ethics are two entirely different dynamics and two entirely different business dynamics. The idea of ethical business relationships, however, was firmly rooted in the interpersonal, one-on-one interactions of the parties involved. The concept of ethics is possible only in personal relationships, not organizational or institutional ones. One of my Russian colleagues, Sergei Filonivich, who is now a management consultant, had previously been a professor at one of the leading universities in Moscow and a partner in several private joint ventures. He described the difference this way:

> Corruption is an act when a decision is made, not in the best interest of the organization, the person, or the country as a whole, but in the interest of a specific group or person. These decisions are made by a bureaucracy. There cannot be corruption between two businessmen. There may be ethical principles that are broken in the relationship. One can lie and another can use you in his business, but that is not corruption. Corruption is a break in morals in the action of the state.

Andrei added, "Corruption is everywhere in this country and in Russian business. Expect it. It is part of the very fabric, the very culture of our country." He made this statement in a very objective way, without any trace of affect or personal responsibility on a personal level.

On the other hand, American managers do not make a distinction between ethics and corruption. To us it's all a matter of accountability for actions, whether those actions are on behalf of an individual, an institution, or the state. Rather than a relationship being at the core of ethical transactions, the contract is at the core of the transaction, as we explore in more detail in this chapter. For Americans the heart of the concept is the transaction, the technical details themselves. To Russians, the heart of the contract is the social and interpersonal relationship between the two parties.

WHAT UNETHICAL BEHAVIOR LOOKS AND SOUNDS LIKE IN BUSINESS TRANSACTIONS

What follows are actions and behaviors defined as unethical by Russians and Americans and their evidence of actions and experiences to support them.

From Russians

The Ethical Indictment: A lack of respect for their technical knowledge

THE SPECIFIC BEHAVIORS:

> Requiring Russian partners to wait for U.S. engineers to assemble transmitting equipment, which the Americans were unable to assemble when they arrived and which Russian engineers assembled quickly and effectively.

> U.S. partners' insistence on writing the specifications for joint venture contracts, rather than asking Russian partners to participate and include what was necessary from their perspective

> A U.S. partners' insistence on using "traditional" channels for marketing and selling popcorn in a popcorn joint venture, rather than listening to the Russian partner's suggestions based on knowledge of the culture and Russian buying patterns

THE ETHICAL INDICTMENT: Russians' feeling slighted or disrespected in business encounters

THE SPECIFIC BEHAVIORS:

> Russians' not feeling listened to regarding technical expertise, peculiarities of the Russian market, or maneuvering through social, political, or bureaucratic relationships

A U.S. partner's spending 3 weeks (without success) trying to negotiate a contract when one phone call by his Russian partner could have done it in an hour

An entrepreneur's not being treated with respect by a clerk in an American company

Many stories from Russian businessmen and entrepreneurs indicating that Americans ought to invest their money more quickly into Russian businesses rather than spending it on trips to Russia to check out potential partners or see for themselves what's going on

THE ETHICAL INDICTMENT: Russians' experiencing a lack of "seriousness" on the part of American companies exploring them as business partners

From Americans

THE SPECIFIC BEHAVIORS:

A Russian businessman's asking for a machine to stamp dates on canned goods. He had just acquired a huge load of outdated canned goods and wanted to restamp them and resell them.

Pervasive extortion by hoodlums and thugs

Payment to individuals in all areas of business and personal transactions just to get the transaction completed.

THE ETHICAL INDICTMENT: Russians act in corrupt and dishonest ways in business dealings

THE SPECIFIC BEHAVIORS:

A Russian city manager's approving a large construction deal then resigning to become president of the construction company

Russian individuals from state enterprises or joint ventures trying to cut separate, private, individual deals

THE ETHICAL INDICTMENT: No understanding of the concept of conflicts of interest

THE SPECIFIC BEHAVIORS:

A Russian's presenting himself in the United States as a big industrialist ready to purchase grain elevators, negotiating the deal, and then completely disappearing

A Russian manager's authorizing the hiring of an accountant in a joint venture, sitting on the paperwork, and 3 weeks after bringing the accountant on board, saying the accountant could not be paid for the 3 weeks unless the American manager paid him out of his own pocket

Russians' signing contracts and then by all appearances simply ignoring them

THE ETHICAL INDICTMENT: Total lack of trustworthiness and integrity

Intrigued with the difference in the perception and implementation of this common and extremely important ideation of ethics in the business context, I wanted to find out what was going on beneath the surface of these cultures that led to such different articulations of ethical decisions and actions.

UNDERSTANDING WHERE CULTURAL DIFFERENCES IN BUSINESS AND ETHICS COME FROM

To gain the proper perspective for a deeper understanding of ethical choices and behaviors by Russians in business transactions, we have to take a large step back. The history and culture of

Russia are ancient and rich, much older than the colonial and post-colonial culture of the United States. I was fortunate to meet Dr. Alexander Kazakov, historian in philosophy of language and visiting scholar at the Bentley College Center for Business Ethics in Waltham, Massachusetts. According to Kazakov, the Russian root for the basis of business ethics is derived from the philosophical concept of *antropos*, a Greek word connoting focus on something beyond your reasoning (Kazakov 1993). The root *an* means "leading upward," coupled with the root *tropos*, or *tropinka*, meaning in Russian "small winding path." In this belief paradigm, belief first comes from logic. Quoting from a popular Soviet song of the 1930s, "We were born to make our dreams reality." Kazakov refers to this as the logic of dreams. Any rational argument is preceded by some kind of faith in dreams. Life is short and brutish. There is another life after this one that we suffer for; belief is over all.

Contrast that faith in the logic of dreams with the American pragmatism derived from the Calvinist tradition of free will, free choice, and accountability, the fundamental elements that fuel the American dream of the good life today. Russians start with a trust in a better life tomorrow, believing that life here and now is worth something only when sacrificed for a better life tomorrow. In the context of business transactions, Russians operate from the mindset of the distinction between what is and what ought to be. This paradigm is translated by pragmatically oriented Americans as irrational thinking or Dostoyevsky's term "the craziness" lived out by the possessed, or the devils.

This underlying philosophy of *antropos* has given way to the behavioral manifestation of *avos* or wishful, magical thinking, which is fundamental to understanding much of the behavior by Russians that Americans label as unethical at worst and maddeningly frustrating at best. In Russian culture, *avos* is shorthand for "Let's just go on and see what happens. Our lives aren't worth anything here, so let's see what happens . . . ." In business interactions it is experienced as, "I wish this would come true," that is, "I wish those Americans would commit their contribution to this wonderful opportunity that I would like to have materialize." As the entrepreneur who founded the radio, television, cable, and paging business in Azov said to me, "It is unethical for Americans to take so long to invest in our businesses when they have the resources." When I asked him whether he believed Americans should be investing more money more quickly into businesses in Russia, he quickly answered, "Yes!" The pragmatism of Americans would counter that it would be an irresponsible action on their part, a choice for which they would be accountable to themselves as well as to their investors and shareholders. Americans would question supporting a deal that does not appear to have the potential for payback and profit to the company and to the shareholder. Pragmatism at work.

MUSIC, MYTH, AND METAPHOR AS MODERN REPRESENTATIONS OF *AVOS*

Music, myth, and metaphor can serve as powerful tools in understanding personal and societal transformation. The philosophical theme of *avos*, or magical thinking—the culture of waiting for life events to act in the way that they must—is beautifully captured in the Russian culture in the following historical account, which has taken on apocryphal proportions in Russian popular culture.

By the end of the eighteenth century, Russia had established a growing fur trading business in the new world of Alaska. In 1799 the Russian-American Fur Trading Company was established, consolidating the resources of the various Russian settlements. In the first decade of the 1800s, the first joint venture, so to speak, between Americans and Russians was initiated through the expeditions of Russians and Aleut Indians coordinated through a New England fur trader, Captain Joseph O'Cain (Rolle 1929). This expedition was formed to hunt sea otter off the southern coasts. It was through this expedition that the Russians became aware of the vast resources of the California coast which was at that time owned and controlled by the Spanish. With increasing glowing accounts of the resources and possibilities of the California coast, Nikolai Rezanov, the Czar's chamberlain who had arrived to inspect the Russian settlements, became more and more interested in the Spanish territories. Although the Russian colonies were well managed under their ruler, Alexander Baranov, disease and starvation began to make life extremely difficult. It was within this context that Rezanov set out to St. Francisco with his ships, the *Juno* and the *Avos*, to trade their cargoes for food and supplies. On arriving at the settlement, the Russian party was courteously received, but the commander of the fort, Commander Arguello, was reluctant to assist the Russians for fear it would be an act of disloyalty. The Russians were beginning to be feared by the Spaniards in that part of the world because Spain was in no political or geographic position to defend its holdings there.

During the period Rezanov was at St. Francisco attempting to make his case for aid for his stricken colonies, he enlisted the aid of and subsequently fell in love with the daughter of the commander. Rezanov's romance with Concepcion Arguello is one of the most famous and most touching in all of California's history. However, it also has become a romantic and legendary underpinning in Russian history and culture. Concepcion, 15 years old at the time, was considered beautiful, and was the acknowledged belle of the province. Rezanov began to speak seriously to Concepcion about the plight of his colonies and the need for aid from her father's post. Soon after his arrival, Rezanov proposed marriage to Concepcion. Although some historians have cynically concluded that this "love story" was heavily biased in favor of securing practical relief for the Russian colonies, most agree that it was indeed a love story.

Concepcion Aguello's father reluctantly agreed to the marriage in spite of the fact that Rezanov was of the Russian Orthodox faith. Soon after the proposal, Rezanov's mission secured a full cargo of foodstuffs, and he sailed to relieve the colony of Sitka. From Sitka, Rezanov traveled across Siberia to return to Russia to seek permission to marry his love. During the journey, however, he was stricken with a fatal illness and never returned to St. Francisco. For many years Concepcion waited for the return of Rezanov, and when he did not return, she became a nun. It was 35 years before she learned the fate of her lover.

This story of Concepcion's waiting for the return of Reza-nov and his ship, the *Avos*, has been immortalized in poems and stories in American literature, the most notable of which is a poem written by Bret Harte in 1896 and included in a collection of poems about turn of the century California (Harte 1896). The Russian opera *Junona and Avos*, by Alekse Rybnikov, has been en-shrined in Russian culture and is, admittedly, the most popular ongoing opera in Russia, a veritable *Cats* of the Russian stage. It is the element of waiting and hoping and yearning in this story, embodied by the very real vessel named *Avos*, that is the cultural touchstone—the perfect metaphor—for the basic philosophical underpinning of Russian culture, which colors and informs the values, thinking, and behavior that lead to ethical perceptions. It is this underlying element of yearning for something else—and the equation with that hope of an impending change in the real-ity of the future—that informs many of the negotiating and con-tractual positions of Russians in business dealings.

CHEKOV AND BUSINESS ETHICS

The Russian playwright Anton Chekov conveyed this philosoph-ical construct of waiting with hope in his play *Uncle Vanya*. At the conclusion of the play the character Sonya speaks as follows:

> Life must go on. And our life will go on, Uncle Vanya. We shall live through a long succession of days and endless evenings. We shall bear patiently the trials fate has in store for us. We shall work for others—now and in our old age—never knowing any peace. And when our time comes we shall die without complain-ing. In the world beyond the grave we shall see that we wept and suffered, that our loss was harsh and bitter, and God will have pity on us. And you and I, Uncle dear, shall behold a life which is bright and beautiful and splendid. We shall rejoice and look back on our present misfortunes with feelings of tenderness, with a smile. And we shall find peace. We shall, Uncle, I believe it with all my heart and soul…. We shall hear the angels, we shall see the sky sparkling with diamonds. We shall see all the evils of this life, all our own sufferings, vanish in the flood of mercy which will fill the whole world. And then our life will be calm and gentle, sweet

> as a caress. I believe that, I do believe it. Poor, poor Uncle Vanya,
> you're crying. There's been no happiness in your life, but wait,
> Uncle Vanya, wait. We shall find peace. We shall find peace.
> (Chekov, *The Major Plays* 1968)

The concept of *avos*, or magical thinking, wishful thinking, coupled with waiting for events to turn out the way we want them
to just because we want them to, is exemplified by the small
string shopping bags that used to be carried by almost everyone,
particularly in large cities. The bags were called *avos* and represented the daily wishful thinking or hope or possibility that during the course of one's day, one may happen upon a line for
some desired goods and with the string bag be in a position to
capitalize on this chance offering (Tourevski and Morgan 1993).

Examples of *avos* thinking in modern business interactions
with Americans include the tendency on the part of Russians to
promise whatever is needed in business dealings with the heart-
felt belief that because they wish it to be so, it will be so. The signing of business contracts with no ability or resources to actually
fulfill them is an example. An entrepreneur from Brattleboro, Vermont, who was engaged in negotiations for three grain elevators
and had signed contracts with his potential partner from Volvo-
grad, finally concluded that the contracts were "really no more
than the minutes of the meeting." I personally was influenced by
this wishful thinking when I listened to my Russian coauthor's
impassioned insistence that "the book *must* be published now"
(after he had delayed the manuscript, causing it to miss the publisher's production cycle) because the timing was right politically
and historically. In this example of wishful thinking, he believed it
would be so because it must be so and he needed it to be so.

This deep belief that the good of the world is out there and
will come to me is deeply fundamental to the interpersonalism of
ethics based on developing and maintaining good personal relations with others and on the part of others. This belief is responsible for the emphasis on personal relations with others and the
requirement in return on the part of others that the emphasis on
personal connections and relationships be crucial. In essence, the
Russian thinking is figuratively and literally: "If I develop the

right relationships deeply enough [Concepcion's love for Reza-nov] my ship [literally the *Avos*] will come in for me." Ironically in this case, as in many situations of Russian-American business dealings, the ship never arrives, and it does not deter Concepcion from waiting in hope for 35 years, meanwhile accomplishing nothing with her life. Many Americans in long-term business re-lationships with Russians have described a similar phenomenon: Russians engage in what is perceived by Americans to be well-intentioned discussions and negotiations, only to "sail" away and either never be heard from again or never deliver on the promised contract. Meanwhile, the business person stands on the metaphorical shore optimistically scanning the horizon, waiting for the sails to appear, only to be left to develop "logical" and "rational" explanations for what has not occurred, ultimately la-beling the interaction, and their partners, unethical.

ARTHUR MILLER AND BUSINESS ETHICS

To understand the analogue to Uncle Vanya in American culture and how it impacts the deeply held beliefs of values that are trans-lated in business interactions, one need only look as far as *All My Sons*, by one of America's premier playwrights, Arthur Miller. The play is about a family in which the father, a manufacturer of air-craft engines, is accused of knowingly sending out 120 engines with hairline fractures, resulting in the deaths of 21 military pilots in World War II. His son, also a pilot, is missing, but the family is convinced he was not flying in a plane with one of the bad engines because he did not fly that particular type of plane (the P-40). After spending a short time in prison, the father is exonerated and re-leased. His partner, however, on whom the blame for this crime of commission is laid, has been sentenced to an extended prison term and disgraced. In his introduction to the play in Arthur Miller's *Collected Plays* (Miller 1957), the author states:

> The crime in "All My Sons" is not one that is about to be commit-ted. There is no question of its consequences being ameliorated by anything Chris Keller or his father can do; the damage has been done irreparably. The stakes remaining are purely the conscience

of Joe Keller [the father] and its awakening to the evil he has done, and the conscience of his son in the face of what consequences he has wrought.

The following is the dialogue when the son confronts the father on the truth:

Chris: I want to know what you did, now what did you do? Explain it to me or I'll tear you to pieces!

Keller (*horrified at his overwhelming fury*): Don't, Chris, don't—

Chris: I want to know what you did, now what did you do? You had a hundred and twenty cracked engine heads, now what did you do?

Keller: If you're going to hang me then I—

Chris: I'm listening. God Almighty, I'm listening!

Keller: You're a boy, what could I do! I'm in business, a man is in business; a hundred and twenty cracked, you're out of business; you got a process, the process don't work you're out of business; you don't know how to operate, your stuff is no good; they close you up, they tear up your contracts, what the hell's it to them? You lay forty years into a business and they knock you out in five minutes, what could I do, let them take forty years, let them take my life away? (*His voice cracking.*) I never thought they'd install them. I swear to God. I thought they'd stop 'em before anybody took off.

Chris: Then why did you ship them out?

Keller: By the time they could spot them I thought I'd have the process going again, and I could show them they needed me and they'd let it go by. But weeks passed and I got no kick-back, so I was going to tell them.

Chris: Then why didn't you tell them...you knew they wouldn't hold up in the air.

Keller: I didn't say that.

Chris: But you were going to warn them not to use them—

Keller: But that don't mean—

Chris: It means you knew they'd crash.

Keller: It don't mean that.

Chris: It means you thought they'd crash.

Keller: I was afraid, maybe—

Chris: You were afraid maybe! God in heaven, what kind of man are you? Kids were hanging in the air by those heads. You knew that!

The consistent and persistent themes of personal accountability because of personal choice for Americans and wishing and hoping for Russians, come through clearly in this passage and are a good example of cultural themes represented in the arts.

These are cultural components that ultimately affect business transactions and the ethical assumptions and behaviors associated with them. The table is a visual summary of some of the cultural considerations revealed through business interactions. I encourage the reader to keep in mind that the United States and Russia are very multicultural societies. The

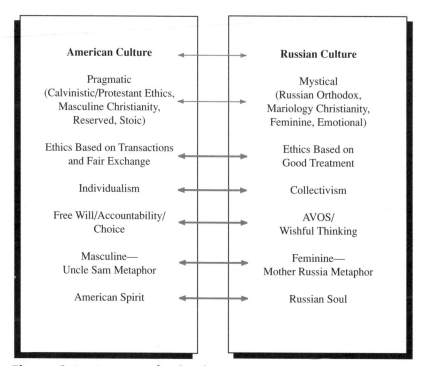

American Culture	Russian Culture
Pragmatic (Calvinistic/Protestant Ethics, Masculine Christianity, Reserved, Stoic)	Mystical (Russian Orthodox, Mariology Christianity, Feminine, Emotional)
Ethics Based on Transactions and Fair Exchange	Ethics Based on Good Treatment
Individualism	Collectivism
Free Will/Accountability/Choice	AVOS/ Wishful Thinking
Masculine— Uncle Sam Metaphor	Feminine— Mother Russia Metaphor
American Spirit	Russian Soul

Figure 3.1 Spectrum of Cultural Dimensions Impacting U.S.–Russian Business Ethics

characteristics identified on the ends of the continuum are in-tended to represent cultural tendencies or characteristics, not characterizations. I draw your attention particularly to the cultural metaphors of spirit and soul.

We speak of American spirit but allude to Russian soul. James Hillman, contemporary psychologist, speaks about the images of the soul exhibiting feminine connotations. Psyche, in the Greek language, "besides being soul, denoted a night moth or butterfly, and a particularly beautiful girl in the legend of Eros and Psyche" (Hillman 1989). Spirit, on the other hand, declares Hillman, is images with light, fire, and wind. Spirit is fast and "it quickens what it touches. Its direction is vertical and ascending; it is arrow straight, knife sharp, powder dry, and phallic. It is masculine, the active principle, making forms, order, and clear distinctions . . . . Soul is vulnerable and suffers; it is passive and remembers" (Hillman 1989). These vivid and contrasting images reflect metaphors for the two cultures that become played out—and misunderstood—at the business table. I remember the poignant comment made by Andrei Manokovsky's wife, Tanya, one night as we spent hours at the small table in their kitchen after dinner, sipping vodka and talking about the changing world. "We and our friends used to sit around this table and talk about politics and freedom. We were all electrified when we were able to read Sakarov's book. Now we sit around this same table, and all we talk about is—*biznez*." On another recent business trip as I drove back from an evening picnic on the beach with a group of entrepreneurs, one of the men spoke passionately about the changes they were all experiencing, the new world they were having to negotiate literally overnight. He spoke eloquently about the deeply felt and emotional aspects of the Russian culture. "Our challenge," he said simply, "is to reinvent the Russian soul for the new millennium." Indeed.

CULTURAL AND ORGANIZATIONAL PROCESS

We are a culture that loves process. We focus on due process in our judicial system. We have made a shrine in our organizations to process management and process engineering and re-engineering, particularly in our technical and manufacturing organizations. So it is not surprising that when you look at how Americans operationalize our values in corporations, it is a recognizable process. Our philosophical and ethical process starts with the fundamental starting point in our culture steeped in Judeo-Christian ideology. Central to this philosophy is the concept of free will, which leads to and implies free choice and, ultimately, accountability for one's choices. If we are empowered by the deepest of forces to choose good or evil, then we and we alone are responsible for the choices that we make. This continuing movement from free will to free choice to accountability implies an ethical philosophy that is process based, that is, accountability for our choices is ongoing as long as the assumption of free will remains intact. What is most interesting, however, is that the results of this ethical process are based on the content of actions, such as specific transactions, specific acts, and specific outcomes—bribery, conflicts of interest, cheating, lying, and misrepresentation—that are specific behavioral outcomes judged by our ethical process.

Russians, on the other hand, have a philosophical perspective that implies a content-based approach to ethics. With their belief in *avos*, what they are contending with in their ethical system is simply "given by the gods," and therefore there is the hope that other things will be given to them. One is ultimately not accountable for what one has had no role in choosing or shaping, a world view that was served well by communism after centuries of rule by the czar and which is reflected in modern business interactions with the west. As Sergei told me, "The ethical problem is that people can [only] feel responsibility about something when they have some power or some way to influence the situation. I can't be responsible about something if I don't have any way to influence the situation." For Russians the ethical formula is reversed: the ethical system is based on content, but the results are evaluated solely on the process of interpersonal relationships.

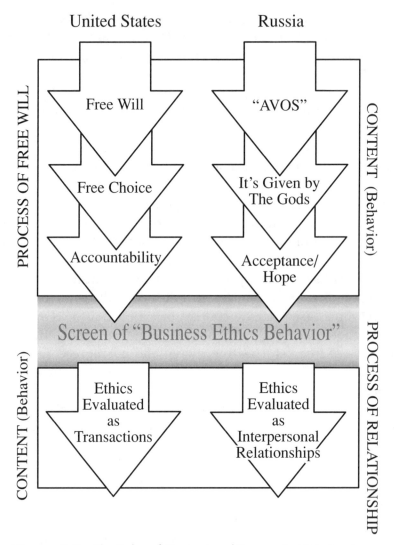

Figure 3.2 The Roles of Content and Process in U.S.–Russian Business Ethics

Let's look at how this difference of assumptions and results works with a specific ethical business dilemma, one of the most common ones, bribery.

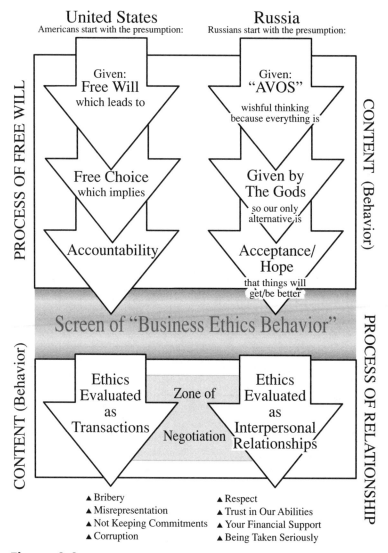

Figure 3.3

We can see how all the elements—culture, history, and philosophical assumptions and interpretation of results—come together in a complex, multifaceted cross-cultural ethical dialogue. The dialogue is unspoken, of course, yet managers are constantly using it to calibrate behaviors and make decisions.

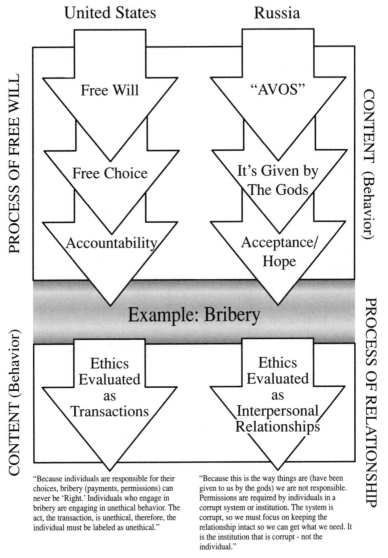

United States   Russia

PROCESS OF FREE WILL

Free Will

Free Choice

Accountability

"AVOS"

It's Given by The Gods

Acceptance/ Hope

CONTENT (Behavior)

Example: Bribery

CONTENT (Behavior)

Ethics Evaluated as Transactions

Ethics Evaluated as Interpersonal Relationships

PROCESS OF RELATIONSHIP

"Because individuals are responsible for their choices, bribery (payments, permissions) can never be 'Right.' Individuals who engage in bribery are engaging in unethical behavior. The act, the transaction, is unethical, therefore, the individual must be labeled as unethical."

"Because this is the way things are (have been given to us by the gods) we are not responsible. Permissions are required by individuals in a corrupt system or institution. The system is corrupt, so we must focus on keeping the relationship intact so we can get what we need. It is the institution that is corrupt - not the individual."

Figure 3.4

As usual, the cartoonists have the last, and most succinct, say with this perfect illustration of how Russians live by the institution yet always acknowledge the individual at the heart of all personal relationships.

THE FAR SIDE   By GARY LARSON

"Listen up, my Cossack brethren! We'll ride into
the valley like the wind, the thunder of our horses and
the lightning of our steel striking fear in the hearts of
our enemies! ... And remember—stay out of
Mrs. Caldwell's garden!"

Figure 3.5 The Far Side (Farworks, Inc. Used by
permission of Universal Press Syndicate. All rights
reserved.

A HOLOGRAPHIC MODEL OF BUSINESS AND ETHICS

This is a wonderful new age in which the fantasy and mystery
of the movie *Star Wars*—one of our cultural metaphors for scientific phenomena that are leading us into new worlds even as we
are unable to fully comprehend them—are becoming the coin of
the realm of our everyday lives. In today's organizations, we
may often feel like Luke Skywalker, watching, even expectantly

perhaps, as a miniature holographic Princess Leia makes an appearance through a beam of light shooting out of R2D2. As we learn more about these scientific phenomena (still debated in the scientific community as a controversial theory or model), the principles of what we call the *new science* are making their way into more accessible literature. There is a movement toward using models from the new science, including the hologram, as metaphors for new ways to lead in organizations (Wheatley 1992; Stacey 1992). What is a hologram, and why should we consider it as a new model for understanding business and ethics in global companies?

Holograms are produced when two waves, such as radio and light waves, intersect and ripple through each other, producing what scientists call *interference*. Any intersection of waves can cause this phenomenon, but because laser light is especially pure, it is especially good at producing these interference patterns. A hologram is produced when a single laser beam is split into two separate beams, and the first beam is made to collide with the second beam. The resulting interference pattern is captured on a piece of film, producing a three-dimensional image. What makes these images so interesting is that any piece of the three-dimensional image can be split off and contains all the elements of the original image (Talbot 1991). This phenomenon has been used as a metaphor by Wheatley as an image for the distribution of complex information in organizations and for the experience of customer service by customers coming in contact with an organization. As an organizational metaphor it has come to represent the ability, and the inevitability, of a single piece of the whole containing the whole.

This is also true when considering business and ethics in global companies. We have traditionally confined the arena of ethics to the universe of philosophy and, in global companies, to cultural considerations of those values. What has become evident to me in my work with companies in many cultures is that there are other "waves" that are part of a holographic ethical system, and each is a part of the whole. If we enter this system at any of the points, we will inevitably see the other waves as well as the whole.

THE HOLOGRAPHIC ELEMENTS

I would like to move our thinking about business ethics away from the sole perspective of duality—of right and wrong, of labeling behavior ethical or nonethical—and begin to put it in the multifaceted perspective of a dynamic, interactive system.

Culturally Specific Considerations

The first wave in our ethical hologram is the one we usually observe when considering business and ethics in global companies, and the one we focus on in this book. When we look at business and ethics solely through this one prism, all we see is difference that must be labeled inferior, inadequate, or not as advanced. As shown in Chapter 5, this wave is extremely useful for simple survival in ethical dilemmas, but it also provides only a piece of the whole.

History of Free Trade and Capitalism

We must consider the history of free trade and capitalism when making our ethical judgments about business interactions in other cultures. For instance, ethical judgments made about Malaysia and Indonesia are harsher than those made about business interactions with the Chinese. Think about how long China as a culture has had a history of trade, even with the recent exclusionary practices of communism. Think about our ethical judgments about Czechoslovakia and Hungary versus the ones we make about Russia, and again put them into the context of an ongoing history of free trade. When the velvet revolution occurred in Hungary, some scientists and professors and even management consultants simply picked up where they left off professionally 33 years earlier. I worked with one senior manager of a new Hungarian management consulting firm who had pumped oil into industrial tankers during the years of communism. For 33 years he fulfilled, with what I considered wonderful grace and equanimity, a very different job from that for which he had been trained. Even with the suppression of communism, there was still accessible cultural memory and experience of engagement in the world, in engagement in trade that was retrieved and updated and refurbished. There was at least a starting point in memory in a critical mass of people to build on. Russia, on the other hand, had no history of free trade extant in any individual or cultural memory when the communist overthrow came.

Degree of Political, Social, or Economic Upheaval

Another wave intersecting into this holographic approach to global companies and business ethics is the degree of political, social, and economic upheaval ongoing in the culture. To what degree is political stability evident? What kind of continuity can be expected and counted on? Specific behaviors that we may label unethical or extremely poor business practices may be born and driven by the unsettling and unsettled day-to-day events that color interpersonal and business interactions. When I was trying to do business in Russia in the confusing and heady days of perestroika, every person with whom I interacted handed me a business card with several layers of their name scratched through, whited out, or written on with new titles. Decisions that are made and behaviors that are observed during times of upheaval cannot be evaluated in the same terms as behaviors from cultures with some ongoing stability. If I am trying to conduct business within a system that is institutionally corrupt and dictatorial, I cannot rely on using that system so I must invent my own system or find creative ways to work around the system and you may interpret that behavior as unreliable, unpredictable, or unethical.

Power Differential in the World Economy

If I am powerful in the world economy, I have the luxury to declare, "We will walk away from the table before we will engage in any behavior that we consider unethical." If I am newly emerging (or even bursting) onto the world scene as a result of these shifting tectonic plates of the new world economy, I do not come to the business transaction with that luxury. "I want to be considered a player in this economy. I need to be there, to be present in it. I may interact with you in any way that I hope will help me catch up with you."

Individual Moral Development

If I am engaging from the point of view of western thinking and behavior, I judge your actions according to my opinions about what constitutes moral development. The literature regarding stages of moral development is deeply embedded in and reflective of linear western thinking which presupposes a disconnected and independently oriented worldview. Major human development theorists have looked at moral development as a set of progressive stages, each building upon the other in a sequential pattern (Kegan 1982; Kohlberg 1984). Similarly, theorists focusing specifically on stages of spiritual development (a specific subset of moral development) also use a progressive stage theory in which moral/spiritual development increases in complexity through time, always building upon and including previous stages (Fowler 1981; Moody 1997). It is not only interesting but crucial to note that other worldviews about moral development prevail in other cultures and have begun to emerge in feminist literature as well. Asian and Native American traditions view the world as a connected whole throughout and not as separate entities appearing in predictable stages. Such a lens must be applied when figuring the whole of the hologram of business and ethics in global companies.

Let's see how these waves work together to form an ethical hologram with one of the most commonly cited ethical dilemmas in global business—bribery.

Instead of navigating cross-cultural ethical situations solely in terms of cultural considerations, we can see how these other complex factors affect the experiences and our judgments of them. If we choose to enter the ethical system on the wave of power differential in the world economy, we can see how that wave is affected by the history of free trade wave, how it is communicated through culturally specific considerations, and the relation to the degree of social,

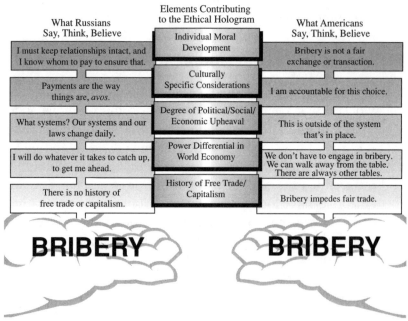

Figure 3.6   Bribery

economic, or political upheaval. If we choose to enter the cross-cultural system on the wave of individual moral development, we can see how the perception that "the most important thing is to keep relationships intact" affects the wave of degree of social and economic upheaval, in which keeping relationships intact allows one to operate in an economic system. No matter where we enter the dialogue (or make judgments) about ethical behavior, we are drawn into the other waves. We cannot enter this dialogue at any point without considering all the other points. Yet even as we struggle to comprehend the whole of a holographic ethical system, we will not understand it all, either the individual pieces or the whole. But we have no choice.

The Layperson's Lament

You understand something and I don't.
You understand that I don't understand, but
You don't understand what it is that I don't understand.

I understand that I don't understand, but
I don't understand what it is I don't understand.
Not only do you not understand what it is I don't understand,
You don't understand how you came to understand
What it is that you understand.
You understand that your understanding is more advanced than
mine,
But you don't understand exactly how it is more advanced,
Nor do you understand how to make yourself simple again like
me.
I understand that your understanding is more advanced than
mine, but
My understanding doesn't feel simple, rather,
It feels chaotic and confused.
I can't begin to explain simply to you
What it is I don't understand
So that you can help me understand it.
You and I have a problem
If I am to come to understand what you understand and
If you are to come to understand what I don't understand.

. . . REPRINTED WITH PERMISSION FROM PETER VAILL, COPYRIGHT 1983.

The holographic ethical system is a broader, more complex approach for navigating cross-cultural ethical differences. In Chapter 4, we start to create an ethical map for cross-cultural navigation that takes into consideration different entry points for an ethical decision (the individual, the organization, and the culture as a whole) and how they are played out against different categories of ethical conflict.

Chapter 4

Creating a Map for Your Cross-Cultural Ethical Navigation

It's All A Swindle

Papa swindles
Mama swindles
Granmama's a lying thief
We're perfectly shameless
but we're blameless
after all its our belief
Nowadays the world is rotten
honesty has been forgotten
fall in love but after kissing—
check your purse to see what's missing
Everyone swindles some
my son's a mooch and so's the pooch

Life's a swindle, yes, it's all a swindle
so get what you can
from your fellow man
Girls and boys today
would rather steal than play
and we don't care
We tell them get your share
Life is short and greed's in season
all mankind has lost its reason
life is good, knock on wood, knock, knock

Shops will swindle
shoppers swindle

every purchase hides a tale
the price is inflated
or regulated
to ensure the store will fail
Wheel and deal and pull a fast one
knowing you won't be the last one
get the goods while they are going
grab the cash while it is flowing
Everyone swindles some
what the heck go bounce a check
Life's a swindle

Politicians
are magicians
who make swindles disappear
The bribes they are taking
the deals they are making
never reach the public's ear
The left betrays, the right dismays
The country's broke and guess who pays
But tax each swindle in the making
profits will be record breaking
Everyone swindles some
so vote for who will steal for you
Life's a swindle

In the summer of 1995, I met with a group of entrepreneurs in the city of Azov, Russia, a small town by the Sea of Azov and an hour from the city of Rostov-on-Don, a city with more than a million people. We met to talk about the obstacles the entrepreneurs faced in getting their businesses started and in trying to navigate the political road maps and obstacles that their country had put in their way. I was there specifically to conduct research on how Russian entrepreneurs—these new businessmen who were emerging in the postperestroika era—defined their own map of ethical constructs in doing business. Although the current businesses of these entrepreneurs were quite diverse, they had all previously worked in some sort of government capacity. Most had been employed by the local factory making military weapons and supplies.

I was impressed with the variety of businesses that these hardworking optimists were launching. The new Russian laws and tax laws were changing so frequently that many of the entrepreneurs were put out of business overnight as a result of the laws and soon after started again. One man had started the first television station in the area. Another was struggling to keep a regional newspaper alive. Another entrepreneur proudly gave me a tour of his rather upscale food markets, which sported canned goods and chocolates from Europe. In addition, he owned a huge sunflower farm and beet and soybean farms. On many occasions, he said, he had slept in the fields to ensure that a potential frost did not endanger his enterprise. Others in the group were involved in traditional trade and importation of consumer goods.

I was obliged by my own ethical code to go through a process known as informed consent. This process tells the interviewees what the research is to be used for and what will happen with the information they provide. It offers an occasion to discuss any issues the interviewees have at the time. Participants are asked to acknowledge their understanding by signing an informed consent form. I distributed a printed informed consent form that had been translated into Russian to each of ten entrepreneurs sitting around a table. Use of the consent forms, intended as a way to acknowledge their rights (in my thinking, at least, and by my cultural standards), backfired.

The forms provoked an unexpected reaction to and accusations of "unethical behavior" on my part. This type of "overdocumentation" was interpreted as a lack of trust on my part. The entrepreneur who made this point about the consent form stated, "All of us here, at one time or another, used to work at the military factory. We all signed a document not to give away the military secrets, and there were only two lines we had to sign."

This example of unethical behavior did not take into consideration any perceived necessity or requirement, legitimate or otherwise, on my part. The behavior, while simply a cultural faux pas by my accounting, was perceived and labeled as unethical solely because of what the interviewees perceived as a lack of trust on my part. In a culture where relationship is everything, documentation is experienced as a lack of trust and therefore determined to be unethical. Recalling how Russians ascribe corrupt behavior to institutions and unethical or ethical behavior to individuals, I could make sense of the interaction. For an American like myself, the idea that being asked to sign such a document would be perceived as unethical behavior seemed slightly ridiculous. However, looking at it through the lens of their culture, I found myself asking, what do documents mean in this culture? In the former Soviet culture what role did documents themselves play in reassurances of conformity? Were the documents evidence of productivity or scornful reminders of meaninglessness? How does that contrast against the perception of documents in the United States as evidence of productivity, vigilance against litigiousness, and comforting reassurance of contractual obligations understood and agreed to? I was shocked to find myself on the receiving end of being labeled unethical. What I needed—and what many managers in similar situations need—is a map or guide for figuring out perplexing or troubling situations.

CREATING THE MAP

The first task in successful ethical navigation is to create a navigational map that helps you understand what kind of behavior you are describing and what kind of label is generally ascribed to that behavior in western business culture.

Even with a good map it can be difficult to maneuver. I live in a rural part of southern Connecticut where the only routes north to south or east to west are twisting, hilly, leafy country roads. Many are confusingly marked with street or road signs that inexplicably change names midroad without warning. Some are marked with old wooden roadpost signs in varying degrees of disrepair and wear from nature. Without a large-print Hagstrom's map of the area and a good map light inside my four-wheel-drive vehicle, I could never have made it from one point to another during the first year I lived there. Today, with the smugness and arrogance that several years' worth of successful navigation brings, I can watch with amusement the vehicles—autos, trade vans, delivery trucks, station wagons, and limo sedans—pulled off on the shoulder of the road, heads bent deeply and intently into a map.

UNDERSTANDING THE BOUNDARIES OF THE MAP

The first step in creating a navigational map for cross-cultural ethics is understanding where the boundaries are. Every individual in every organization does not necessarily have trouble or difficulty in all aspects of navigation. Every global company does not find their dilemmas and difficulties in every quadrant.

The first step in using a map to help us figure out where we are in the coordinates of cross-cultural ethics, where we experience the most dilemmas as an individual or an organization, is to figure out whether we are looking at a situation through an individual's lens, an organization or company's lens, or the global cultural lens at large. Then we'll try to understand whether we are talking about something that is clearly illegal, fraudulent, and corrupt. Is it considered "unethical" by our cultural standards and values or questionable practices? Is it considered unfair from our capitalistic perspective and our Judeo-Christian point of view of contracts and fairness, or is it considered inappropriate from an intercultural, multicultural, or interpersonal relationship perspective—it is not just "how we do things here." In thinking through these questions, we can be in a better position to understand what we are dealing with, how important it is to the individual manager or the organization, and the choices for dealing with it.

Cross-cultural ethics is a poorly mapped domain. Our early maps, just like the early maps of a country, are crudely drawn, with little detail, with too much emphasis in some areas and too little in others. The boundaries are unclear, and certainly many cultures often lay claim to the same geography. Well-meaning corporate codes do not necessarily help. As the Whirlpool Code mentioned in Chapter 1 states: "No employee of this company will be called upon to do anything in the line of duty that is morally, ethically, or legally wrong." When managers are dealing with only U.S. laws and generally accepted ethical practices, that may be clear. When a manager is trying to navigate in cultures where laws are constantly changing and where business practices shift solely on the basis of the personality of the individual involved, it may not be so clear.

It is no longer acceptable for travelers in a global world to shrug their shoulders and sigh that figuring out the ethical terrain is simply too difficult. We have lived too long doing business with the belief, the escape clause if you will, that this business of cross-cultural ethics and business negotiations is too complex and that we would, one day, figure it all out. Most texts used in business ethics courses at the graduate level allude to cross-cultural ethics, usually with the caveat that the whole affair is complex and needs further study.

Rushworth Kidder, founder and president of The Institute for Global Ethics in Camden, Maine, has proclaimed that based on worldwide research, a set of eight core values has emerged upon which there is apparent global consensus: love, truthfulness, fairness, freedom, unity, tolerance, responsibility, and respect for life (Kidder 1994). However, when pressed regarding global consensus about the *meaning* of these vibrant concepts and the subsequent behaviors and actions resulting from them, he admits that things get problematic.

With the increase in globalization and the increase in the number of individuals involved in global business, we can't put it off any longer.

Like geographical maps, our cross-cultural ethical map has two sets of coordinates to help us locate where we are. A map, a navigational device, is used to accomplish the following:

- Provide a way to understand the type of dilemma we are encountering and the kind of language that best describes what is happening.
- Help managers understand the scope of the "player" in the situation. Is it an individual experiencing a dilemma or causing ethical discomfort, an organization as a whole, or a culture as a whole?
- Help managers figure out and understand what types of dilemmas they tend to encounter in their particular day-to-day situations and the individual and organizational implications for leadership, policies, and structure.

The Horizontal Coordinates

The horizontal coordinates are lenses we use to map the point of view of the ethical decision maker.

Lens 1: The Individual Lens

This lens is the voice of the person who is asking questions or making decisions—the individual "actor" in the global business drama. On the ethical map it is the viewpoint of the person who is either perceiving an individual other than him or herself as "unethical" or who is being viewed by another individual in another culture as "unethical."

The Ethical Map

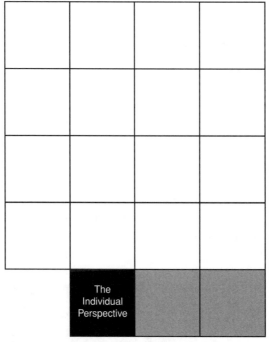

Figure 4.1 The Individual Perspective

Lens 2: The Organizational Lens

This is the lens through which the organization—its policies, practices, official decisions—is the decision maker.

Lens 3: The Global and Cultural Lens

This is the ethical perspective determined by the specific culture as a whole or a combination of cultures referred to as *global*.

The Vertical Coordinates

Working in many cultures over the years and consulting with managers, leaders, employees, and executives in various companies, I have found, that the word *ethics* is used indiscriminately for differ-

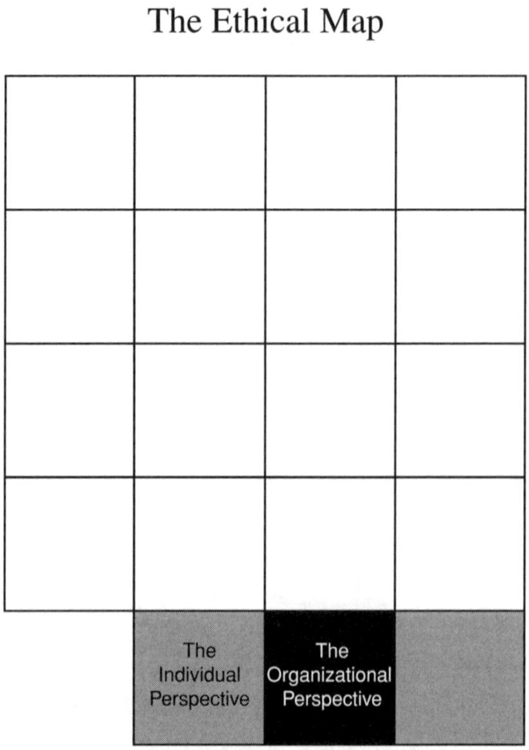

The Ethical Map

Figure 4.2 The Organizational Perspective

The Ethical Map

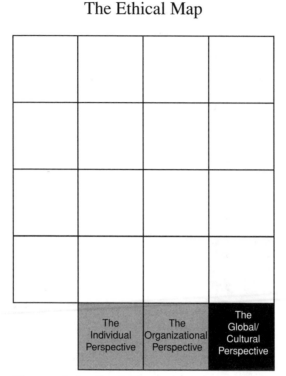

Figure 4.3 The Global and Cultural Perspective

ent types of behavior, perceptions, expectations, and interpretations of intent. Let's look at four types of ethical transgressions—from the most blatant (and well defined) to the most subtle.

Ethics as Illegality; Fraud or Corruption

This is the category that is easiest to define and to which most attention is paid. It is easy to define others' behaviors as illegal or fraudulent when held in relief against our own domestic laws. We even feel some sense of reassurance in the cross-cultural arena when we view actions by other cultures that we believe violate the clear guidelines of the Foreign Corrupt Practices Act, because these actions are clearly defined and therefore clearly labeled.

Fraud is big business internationally and its nature is constantly changing. Corporate restructurings, political instability

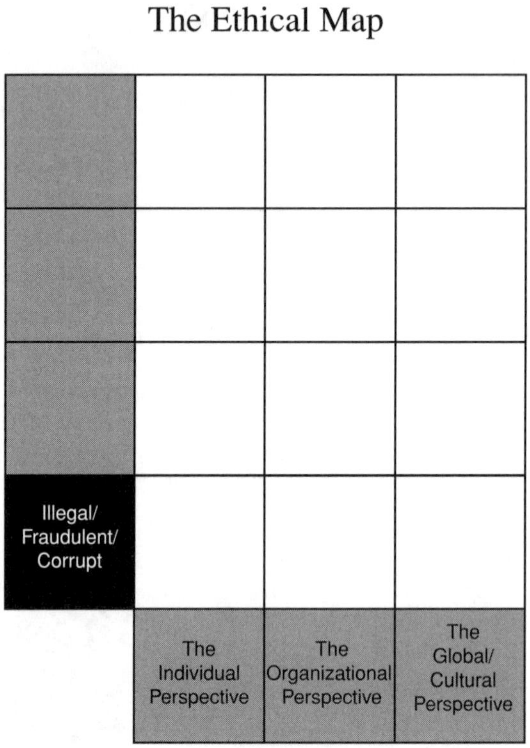

The Ethical Map

Illegal/ Fraudulent/ Corrupt			
	The Individual Perspective	The Organizational Perspective	The Global/ Cultural Perspective

Figure 4.4 Ethics as Corruption, Fraud, and Illegalities

in various areas of the world and rapid technological advances are among the factors giving rise to new and more complex mechanisms for fraud. According to the KPMG study, two of the major factors affecting the level of fraud are society's weakening values and economic pressures. There is less ambiguity in finding a "slot" or an ethical "home" for these actions. At the same time we are pointing our fingers and labeling, we can sigh with relief that at least *some* things are clear, and each is tied to specific legal structures. "People are very inclined to set moral standards for others" (Elizabeth Drew 1987).

Ethics as Personal and Organizational Values

This category is the most problematic because it is the category that taps into our deepest cultural, spiritual, and personal beliefs about basic rightness. Unethical behaviors in business interactions violate our deeply held personal norms and beliefs regarding important values about right and wrong *as we learned them* in our own culture and from our own families. Nonetheless, as mentioned previously, The Institute for Global Ethics in Camden, Maine, contends that there are eight core values upon which all cultures base their ethical constructs: love, truth, freedom, fairness, unity, tolerance, responsibility, and respect for life (Kidder 1994). A hopeful message, however, is that at the next level of how each culture interprets the meaning of those values in the implementation of business practices, the values become problematic as guidelines or road markers. This is the category in which it is not a question of right or wrong or legal or illegal, but of right versus right.

The Ethical Map

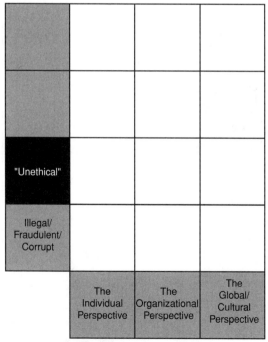

Figure 4.5 Ethics as What We Normally Perceive as Values

Ethics as Unfairness

This category on the vertical map coordinates comes directly from our deeply steeped economic and political tradition of capitalism, a tradition in which we are so completely embedded that we lose the perspective of its direct effect on our day-to-day lives and assumptions about business interactions. Capitalism is founded so squarely on the bedrock of the notion of contracts—exchange of goods and services for agreed upon compensation—that we tend to lose sight of its underlying and encompassing theme. In U.S. organizations, for example, the assumption of fairness is played out in our policies of equal opportunity, merit systems, and other organizational practices designed to ensure that each individual has equal access to bettering his or her individual condition in the overall system.

Thomas Donaldson (1996) professor at The Wharton School of the University of Pennsylvania in Philadelphia, writes about

The Ethical Map

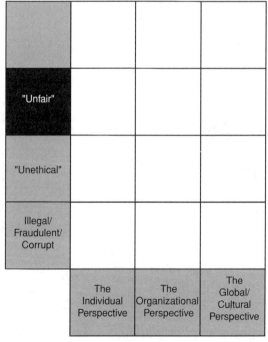

Figure 4.6   Ethics as Unfairness

business ethics as social contracts, again bringing the fundamental concept of contracts into assumptions about cross-cultural ethical decision making (see Chapter 3 as an example of how this idea of contracts comes into play in a specific cross-cultural business transaction with Russians and Americans). The notion of contracts also comes out of our western Judeo-Christian tradition of free will and its accompanying accountability. Our cultural assumption is that because we are the products of the gift of free will, the implied contractual result of that free will is our obligation to use our choices wisely and to be personally accountable for them.

Ethics as Inappropriateness

The last category consists of our cultural judgments based on our assumptions about interpersonal relationships and common business practices. Sociologists have long labeled these types of assumptions and behaviors *folkways*. It is in this category that judgments about the role of women in business relationships and interactions and the treatment of women in general come into play. Here we also find issues based in what Geert Hofstede, researcher, author, and professor at the European Institute for Advanced Studies in Management refers to as *power distance*, or what the nature of the professional and social relationship between managers and employees should be (Hofstede, 1984). These are issues of personal power, class, and equality of treatment. Issues of what U.S. organizations frequently refer to as *empowerment* come under scrutiny here, as do our very clear dictates of what is right and appropriate organizational cultural behavior.

We can now lay out both the horizontal and vertical coordinates of our ethical map and see the landscape we are attempting to navigate.

FRAUD AND CORRUPTION AND THE INDIVIDUAL

Think about the headlines that have riveted our attention over the last few years: Joe Jett, the trader at Kidder Peabody who brought

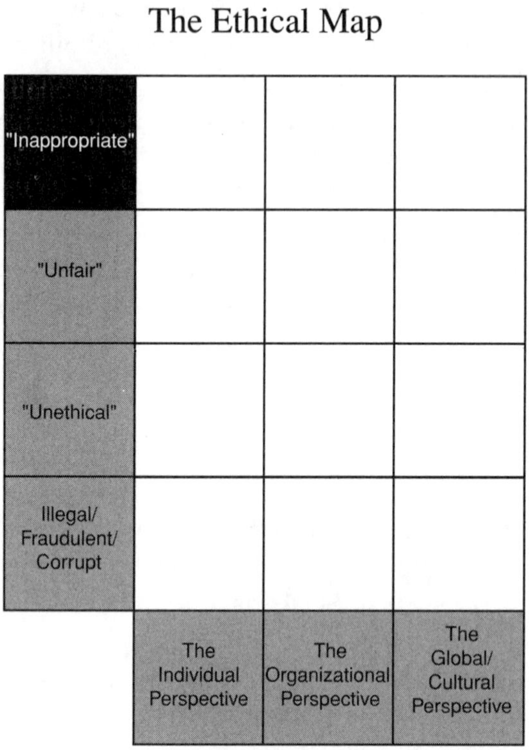

The Ethical Map

	The Individual Perspective	The Organizational Perspective	The Global/ Cultural Perspective
"Inappropriate"			
"Unfair"			
"Unethical"			
Illegal/ Fraudulent/ Corrupt			

Figure 4.7   Ethics as Inappropriateness

the investment house to its knees through a series of covered-up big deals gone bad. Nicholas W. Leeson, the 28-year-old Bad Boy of Baring's whose billion-dollar-plus losses in trades collapsed the 150-year-old British trading bank. In addition to the headlines, however, are the countless acts of fraud and thievery that individuals commit, such as the secretary at a New York multinational bank who forged cash advances under her boss's signature to help tide her over during some tight financial times. One of the first things that usually comes to mind when we think of unethical behavior is the fraud that is committed by an individual.

Fraud has a long and rich history. Over the centuries we have developed a rich vocabulary for it: trickery, chicanery, monkey business, hanky-panky, funny business, flimflam, cozenage, hoodwinking, swindling, pettifoggery, pulling the wool over one's eyes, knavery, duplicity, artful dodging. We describe individuals who act in this way as imposters, pretenders, masqueraders, quacks, charlatans, fakes, phonies, fourflushers, cheats, swindlers, con men, and bamboozlers. In business transactions, we describe both the individuals and the behavior as unethical.

The Statistics of Fraud

The statistics around the depth and scope of fraud in U.S. companies are staggering. The Association of Certified Fraud Examiners, which studies and quantifies fraud in business institutions, defines fraud as a situation in which a client or a prospect intentionally deceives an organization to benefit themselves by the increase of credit facility, modification, or better terms. In the banking industry alone the findings of the 2 1/2-year study showed that losses totaled $15 billion in actual fraud losses, ranged from $22 to $25 billion, and represented 12 different major industry groups. Fraud is not restricted to the rank and file. The study showed that 62% of inventory shrinkage caused by employees, was committed by company supervisors. Nearly 48% of U.S. workers admitted to taking unethical or illegal actions in the past year. The study also showed that the average organization loses more than $9 a day per employee per day to fraud and that the average organization loses about 6% of it is total annual revenue to fraud committed by its own employees. It costs U.S. organizations more than $400 billion annually. So it should not be a surprise to us to learn that when U.S. companies spend money to protect themselves against the unethical behavior of their own employees and against other companies' unethical behavior, 99% of all the funds they spend are directed toward detecting that 1% of "bad apples" in the organizations (Stephen E. Silver interview with author, March 13, 1997).

Stories of individual fraud can be spectacularly compelling. High-profile stories that make international headlines, such as that of Nick Leeson from Baring's Bank, capture all of us in a freeze frame of looking into our own souls and psyches and asking, "Would I have done that? Would I have been *tempted*? Given the opportunity, would I have played games on paper showing enormous institutional profits while skimming off a great deal for myself? Would I have been tempted with stakes as high as those?"

One of the most common forms of corruption cited by managers working cross culturally is what we would label bribes—extra payments made simply to execute what we would consider normal transactions in the course of ordinary business. When listening to the stories of managers involved in countries where "bribery" is a way of life, one of the key things I heard repeatedly was a sense of frustration at having to pay above and beyond an extra premium simply to accomplish things that were required in the normal course of business.

John Klein is a business development explorationist with Union Texas Petroleum. He has worked 15 years in the exploration business in the oil industry. Starting with Cities Service Company and then with Union Texas, John has worked in Latin America, London, North Africa, Europe, Jakarta, Indonesia, Brazil, and Venezuela. He described common examples of bribery and corruption while working in other countries, especially Indonesia, where it was "constantly getting something for doing nothing . . . . People knew they couldn't be fired, and there was nowhere in the organization for them to go, so why not make some demands."

Michael Morgan is a lifelong senior career chemical engineer with Conoco. Working around the world from Dubai to Cairo, the North Sea to Trinidad, Michael has built large natural gas processing plants both onshore and offshore. As the manager for a significant part of the topsides of the Heidrun Tension Leg Platform built for offshore in Norway in the early 1990s, Michael was responsible for coordinating teams of engineers from around the world to build the world's largest natural gas platform, get it into the water, and ship it to its location in the North Sea.

At one point in his career, Morgan worked on a project in which the main contractor was a fabrication yard in southern Italy. During the course of the project, one of the Statoil managers rented a car and was driving to the contracting site when he stopped to use the phone and have a meal. When the manager returned, the car was gone. Through alternative transportation the manager arrived at the fabrication yard after several hours and explained what had happened. The manager of the fabrication yard picked up the phone and began yelling into it. When he finished he told the Statoil manager, "Your car and all the possessions you had in it will be at your hotel in 15 minutes." Apparently it was not an uncommon practice to hijack goods in this way.

In another Conoco example, Morgan related that Statoil, the state-owned oil company Den Norske Oije Selscap, needed to get materials from one side of Norway to another and had to pay a substantial sum of money. Morgan's advice was to keep somebody on-site on these kinds of projects at all times.

John Klein says of Nigeria, "You can't even get into or out of the airport without paying a fair chunk of money."

Devon Archer came to Vietnam as the Manager of Citibank's Direct Investment Sector with an unusual and emotionally powerful history. Devon, now 23 years of age and a graduate of Yale University, always had an interest in Vietnam and as a history major at Yale studied American interests in there. Devon's interest in Vietnam was more than just scholarly or academic. His father had been a wounded Vietnam veteran. Right after he graduated from Yale, Devon took a trip to Asia and spent most of his time in Vietnam. "It was at the time that Vietnam was just opening up," recalls Devon. Upon graduating from Yale, he considered several offers and decided to work for a company that would bring him to Vietnam; eventually he moved to Citibank. Because Devon understands more about the culture of Vietnam, he understands the depth of the graft and corruption there. For the most part, he is philosophical in his acknowledgment of it. However, one incident in particular made him extremely frustrated:

> I wrote a Citibank Investment Guide. It was a big deal and nicely done—a 65-page bound book with color photographs. It specifically described the environment, provided marketing tools for

Stan Schrager is senior vice president of the Chase Manhattan Bank. A veteran of 27 years at the bank and of worldwide assignments that have put him squarely at the center of the growth and expansion of the global bank, Stan has been involved in many situations that do not seem clear cut and that do seem to be at odds with practices in the United States. Stan described some of these human resource practices that put the company in somewhat of a dilemma regarding the ethical behavior of the organization: "We had a situation in Italy, with people submitting bogus expenses to supplement their salary. When employees go over there they are paid on the scale of the economy and frequently feel that they are taking a pay cut. It's a disincentive for being over there. So it was a common practice to submit these expense reports to compensate their salary." Other kinds of organizational practices that seem to skirt the edges of ethical behavior, certainly in Italy, include paying bonuses and interest-free loans in Brazil:

> It's all perfectly legal. It was a compensation scheme with Chemical prior to the merger with Chase, and it had to be reevaluated. In Chile one of the common practices was to pay people offshore, which made it nontaxable. Now, the accounting firm Price Waterhouse said it was clearly a common practice, but they wouldn't put it in writing as being acceptable. Other kinds of compensation schemes, including companies putting benefit programs into place—like special cars, housing allowances—they're all nontaxable, but they're perfectly legal. But over time they become much more expensive.

Mike Morgan of Conoco remembers the time that he was dealing with customs agents on the large Phoenix Park Gas Processors Project in Trinidad:

> The agents, who had to approve our imported equipment and materials coming in through the dock near our project site, had a shack right beside the dock. We had a good relationship with them and then one day one of the managers in the customs agency said that he would like to have a TV. Now, for us that's

obviously not a big expense. Would it help facilitate our customs shipments? That's what was obviously implied. Our way around that dilemma was to buy a television, but to put it in a common waiting room so that all of the agents and other employees who were there would have access to it.

I'd expected to hear stories about the increasingly prevalent and powerful Russian thugs when eliciting stories of unethical behavior, and those stories certainly came to light in many ways. Susan, a young American at a Russian-American telecommunication joint venture described paying protection money to hoodlums and thugs more as a practical element required to do business than behavior that's unethical. Susan differentiated the run-of-the-mill payments made to various outlaw groups just to stay in business safely from payments made to the state hoodlums in Tumin, a city where they had a large operation. The latter payments were required to allow the telecommunication joint venture permission to run its telecommunication wires over the property. Even though the property was state owned, the permissions were paid to private individuals. Additional payments were made on an ongoing basis for buying a car, obtaining a driver's license, or just about any type of personal or business activity imaginable.

Fraud, Corruption, Crime, and the Culture

We have a tendency to label entire cultures as unethical because they are doing things that we label as illegal, fraudulent, or corrupt. Every few years I receive a letter from some "high official" in Nigeria asking for my "help" in getting large sums of cash out of the country—with a nice cut for me to reward my cooperation. I have no idea how I got on this list. I received the first letter almost 10 years ago, when I was working out of my small office next to the general store in a very small town in Vermont. Over the years, the English has become slightly better, but the illegal and corrupt intentions have not. Although the name of the "high official" and the sender of the letter change, along with the reason for the cash being at hand and the dollar amount, they all read like the most recent one I received, in spring of 1998:

CONFIDENTIAL
This Letter Is Made Only for the Under-Designated or Titled Personnel

From: Abdul Mohammed Wase (Jnr.)
Telefax: 234-42-457151, 450260
Attn: The President/Director

Sir.

Introduction
I am Mr. Abdul M. Wase (jnr.) the heir and son of late Colonel Mohammed Wase. Until the time of my father's death in a plane crash at Jos airport here in Nigeria, now renamed Mohammed Wase airport, he was the governor of Kano state, Nigeria.

In a will message made by my father and his emergency letter of instructions which he has always left for me or my mother, he drew my attention to his strong room in our country home (ie village) where he kept a total sum of $77 million used cash in a security trunk. However, the whole currency notes were defaced or coated with a substance that will not alter its value. My late father did that to safe guard the funds.

In his instructions he directed that I should contact a security and finance company in Abidjan with the contact address and phone which he left for me. It is the security company that will reinstate or wash the us currency note to its original. He further instructed that I should contact a reliable and trustworthy partner overseas who can assist me to move this funds into an account abroad after which I will invest the funds wisely.

Source Of Funds

The Aforementioned sum was made when my father was governor and as an oil royalist from the crude oil in our land.

It is based on the instructions of my late father that I am contacting you and to solicit for your total confidence and trustworthiness so that you can assist me to execute this transaction perfectly. Also note that no risk is involved in this transaction but you have to maintain utmost secrecy hence nobody else knows about this deal except you, my mother, and myself.

Conclusion

Sir, if you are willing to assist me, I will like you to call or send fax to me through telefax numbers above for detailed information.

Previous letters have offered me the grand sums from $17 million if I will send them by fax my bank account numbers or other "particulars on my company letterhead." Interestingly, enough individuals have taken these hucksters up on their offer that full-page ads of warnings not to do so have appeared regularly in the *New York Times* and the *Wall Street Journal*.

Unethical behavior often is attributed not to the individual or to the organization, but to the culture at large. At the time I talked to Chris Burbach, she was vice president of international programs at the EF foundation. She described some of her experiences in India while she was doing her dissertation research and living there for 6 months:

India's a very bureaucratic country. Doing the dissertation, the hardest part was having to deal with that bureaucracy as such an entrenched part of the culture. The head of the nutrition department at Baroda University didn't help much. I had to do it myself. I found a Gudung woman in the department who helped me. It was plainly evident that I could pay my way through the university to get help, and I didn't pay people. I might have done a lot better if I had. Today I might. I might offer a large "contribution" to the university or find some way to let it be known that people were better off because I was there and using their help. I'd be a lot smarter today.

John Klein, the explorationist from Union Texas Petroleum, talked about some of his experiences in Indonesia in getting approvals from the military personnel in a Union Texas exploration area:

The hand is always out looking for a payoff. It's just part of the culture. I can understand the need for payoffs because they are grossly underpaid—at the same time we're spending huge sums of money to get operations done as quickly and as efficiently as we can. You always have the pressure of planning way ahead because we know we're going to run into that. That's something that's not as common in the developed world. At every level you just assume that someone's going to get something out of it. The sums of money we're talking about aren't large sums of money. It's pocket change actually. They don't want a lot of money. They just get a little bit from everybody. If you get stopped for a traffic violation, you just pay. It amounts to $20, $40, $60 a day while it's going on. Anytime anyone wants to get on the plane, whether they're twin engines or others, you pay. You get out to the field and they could bump you for military people. Then you have to wait 2 days for the next flight. It was either charter an aircraft, which is very expensive, or you give them a little bit of money to get on the airplane. It's a constant thing. It actually adds up more to saving time than spending money, but it does add up even though the total amount of money isn't much. It's the time, the domino effect—it throws everything off.

Alain Batty is Executive Director for Asia Pacific and New Market Support for the Ford Motor Company. He has worked in Australia, New Zealand, Taiwan, India, and China. A few years ago he was President of Operations in Spain. Before that he was a senior manager in Belgium for 20 years. Comments Batty:

In Europe—Spain—people like to make gifts. In Spain, we're the fifth largest company, so we're sent gifts by everyone. At Christmas time it's a real problem. People eventually begin to understand you don't need to receive all these gifts to do business, but you can't really send them back. For instance, the books that we receive we give to the libraries. We get a lot of food, like good hams. We give those away. The way you handle these things makes a difference about how you perform in the country.

THE CORRUPTION PERCEPTION INDEX

An international organization, Transparency International, based in Berlin, issues an annual report on corruption. Countries around the world are listed from least to most corrupt given a certain set of criteria. The corruption perception index (CPI) is based on seven international surveys of business people, political analysts, and the general public and reflects *their* perception of corruption in 52 countries. Countries are ranked from least corrupt to most corrupt on an annual basis.

Transparency International Perception Index 1997

Rank	Transparency International Corruption Perception Index 1997	Score 1997 (Max. 10.00)	Score 1996 (Max. 10.00)	Number of Surveys Used in 1997	Variance in 1997 Between Surveys
1.	Denmark	9.94	9.33	6	0.54
2.	Finland	9.48	9.05	6	0.30
3.	Sweden	9.35	9.08	6	0.27
4.	New Zealand	9.23	9.43	6	0.58
5.	Canada	9.10	8.96	5	0.27
6.	Netherlands	9.03	8.71	6	0.23
7.	Norway	8.92	8.87	6	0.51
8.	Australia	8.86	8.60	5	0.44
9.	Singapore	8.66	8.80	6	2.32
10.	Luxemburg	8.61	-----	4	1.13
11.	Switzerland	8.61	8.76	6	0.26
12.	Ireland	8.28	8.45	6	1.53
13.	Germany	8.23	8.27	6	0.40
14.	United Kingdom	8.22	8.44	6	1.43
15.	Israel	7.97	7.71	5	0.12
16.	USA	7.61	7.66	5	1.15
17.	Austria	7.61	7.59	5	0.59
18.	Hong Kong	7.28	7.01	7	2.63
19.	Portugal	6.47	6.53	5	1.02
20.	France	6.66	6.96	5	0.60
21.	Japan	6.57	7.05	7	1.09
22.	Costa Rica	6.45	-----	4	1.73
23.	Chile	6.05	6.80	6	0.51
24.	Spain	5.90	4.31	6	1.82
25.	Greece	5.35	5.01	6	2.42
26.	Belgium	5.25	6.84	6	3.28
27.	Czech Republic	5.20	5.37	5	0.22
28.	Hungary	5.18	4.86	6	1.66
29.	Poland	5.08	5.57	5	2.13
30.	Italy	5.03	3.42	6	2.07
31.	Taiwan	5.02	4.98	7	0.76
32.	Malaysia	5.01	5.32	6	0.50
33.	South Africa	4.95	5.68	6	3.08
34.	South Korea	4.29	5.02	7	2.76
35.	Uruguay	4.14	-----	4	0.63
36.	Brazil	3.56	2.96	6	0.49
37.	Romania	3.44	-----	4	0.07
38.	Turkey	3.21	3.54	6	1.21
39.	Thailand	3.06	3.33	6	0.14
40.	Philippines	3.05	2.69	6	0.51
41.	China	2.88	2.43	6	0.82
42.	Argentina	2.81	3.41	6	1.24
43.	Vietnam	2.79	-----	4	0.26
44.	Venezuela	2.77	2.50	5	0.51
45.	India	2.75	2.63	7	0.23
46.	Indonesia	2.72	2.65	6	0.18
47.	Mexico	2.66	3.30	5	1.18
48.	Pakistan	2.53	1.00	4	0.47

The rank of a country is derived from survey and studies reflecting the views of country experts, businesspeople, and/or the general public. It does not reflect the view of Transparency International.

Figure 4.8 Transparency International Perception Index 1997. Reprinted with permission of Transparency International.

ETHICS AS DEEPLY HELD VALUES FOR THE INDIVIDUAL AND THE ORGANIZATION

Scott Thomas is vice president for Pacific sourcing for Reebok and has lived in Asia and worked in the footwear industry for more than 20 years. Reebok and other footwear manufacturers do not own any factories directly in Asia. Rather, they have long-term exclusive arrangements with suppliers on site there. The companies do not manage the factories directly; however, Reebok's policies and preferences play a strong role in how the factories are actually run. Scott is well aware of the growing controversies surrounding labor practices in Asia and has been quite open about areas in which they need to improve.

Scott's work with Reebok provides an excellent example of behaviors labeled as "unethical" that hit directly at the values held and professed by Reebok that come directly out of our western, U.S. culture. Sociologists have labeled these values as our norms, the internal guidebook that is hardwired into us and provides information for how we live our lives. One of those values is an assumption that people have a right to be treated well and not be exploited, values that have been articulated publicly by Reebok and the company policies. Making the bridge from ethical values to ethical behavior, especially in a very different culture, is fraught with pitfalls, misunderstandings, and missed opportunities.

Sensitive to the accusation that workers in their supplier factories in China were being made to work inhuman hours, Scott investigated the situation:

> We thought we had pretty good control over the amount of hours that were being reported as worked by individuals. When we were doing our auditing—the monitoring of the factory—and asking for data, we got to digging into this a couple of years ago. It turns out that there were many ways to interpret what we were asking for in terms of work hour information. The average by department may have been 60 hours, but 20 people out of maybe 1,000 in that department could have worked 80 hours. It was the 60 hours number that was reported. The same things on work hours. We looked into how the hours were recorded. The payroll

records in some of our large factories are all done manually. You look at the overtime sheets and it's just a scratch, a tick mark—ten, one, three. There's no easy way for a supervisor to determine that this worker on this sewing line has already worked up to 60 hours. They couldn't red flag that easily enough, to say who's only worked 55 hours and can work some overtime, and who's already worked 60 hours and shouldn't work overtime. The record keeping was simply not developed well enough. These are the sorts of things you think you've got a good handle on because your reports look great. But if you monitor it and talk to people on the line, we find out we actually do have a problem with some misinterpretation.

Scott Thomas and Reebok are trying to run a business that reflects the personal and organizational value of respect for the individual. In this instance, the respect comes in the form of not exploiting a worker who easily could be exploited by being lost in a crowd or lost in unsophisticated paperwork. Even if 60-hour work weeks are considered normal in another culture, the values we claim as our own are seen as deep enough and important enough to this company that they truly attempt to run a business in alignment with them.

ETHICS AS UNFAIRNESS

We are a culture, and especially a business culture, that is based on the principles of capitalism. One of the prominent foundations of capitalism is the idea of the contract. In business negotiations the concept of a contract is exactly that—a contract for services, a contract for fees in exchange for services. However, Thomas Donaldson in his latest book, *Business Ethics as Social Contracts* (1998), has indicated that there is also the perspective of looking at ethics as a social contract between the individual in the culture and the culture at large and between cultures.

The word *ethics* is so often used as language to describe behavior that through our cultural lens and perspective can be described simply as unfair behavior from our capitalistic point of view.

Let's go back to Susan, the young U.S. woman living in Moscow who was the marketing manager for the large American-Russian telecommunication joint venture. One of the examples she gave to describe unethical behavior was that her landlady in Moscow raised her rent every month—and by a substantial margin. Susan's lament was that it just didn't seem right for someone to be able to do that. When she had taken the apartment, they had agreed on a certain amount as the rent and for a certain period of time, yet the landlady would raise the rent every month, threatening Susan with eviction if she didn't comply. Susan felt like she had no recourse but to keep paying or to move every month. Susan described that as an unethical way to do business. A small, everyday occurrence, not a big national event, not a big event with millions of dollars at stake, but a small interaction that she faced everyday. In essence, what Susan was reacting to was the unfairness of it all. Yet the label, the language used, was the word *ethics*.

John Klein, the explorationist from Union Texas Petroleum, commented on this aspect of fairness on the individual level. John was referring to what he described as the attitude of constantly getting something for nothing in the Indonesian culture. At the time, he was supervising 19 people. Twelve or 13 of them were nationals, and the rest were expatriates. Says John:

> That idea of always getting something for nothing—that's at odds with the way I am and who I am. I'm a strong believer in working hard and earning your pay, and if you work harder, you'll get more pay. You need to be dedicated enough and not just be fed. Our standard of living is light years ahead of theirs. They know you're not there for long. In the big picture you'll only be here for 2 to 3 years. Some of them prey on outsiders' generosity. It didn't seem right to me and it doesn't seem fair that they don't work as hard as I think they should.

John was dealing with the concept of fairness and unfairness, coming straight out of our western capitalist thinking of contract-based interactions in business.

FAIRNESS AND THE GLOBAL PERSPECTIVE

Some of the managers I spoke with had things to say about fairness that plugged directly into the cultural and global aspect. Chris Burbach, previously the Vice President of U.S. Language Travel Programs for the international, Boston-based EF Foundation said:

> In some of the countries I've worked in, for example, Armenia, you have to pay people off. The expectation is you give some money to someone and you get something done. Previously, when a senior manager with another international exchange organization, I was involved in a program called Freedom Support Exchange Programs. We were offering scholarships to the U.S. for teenagers from Armenia. They had to take tests and we interviewed them. It was very competitive. It was very difficult for the parents of these students to understand that we would be selecting these participants based on the tests and the interviews. They offered all kinds of things for us to pick their kids for the travel scholarships. The day that we announced the winners was unbelievable. A thousand people crowded into the courtyard. It was an opportunity of a lifetime for these kids and their families. It was assumed though, that some kids would win because of who their parents were. It took a lot of finessing to work all this through. People were incredibly loud and angry—why weren't their kids chosen or offered the program scholarships! One area that we visited had been especially hard hit by an earthquake. We went out to a school there and we interviewed the kids there. Afterwards, the people in the school, the families and the community, provided a huge feast. Here in the U.S., we're so used to merit that we take it for granted. There they offered us cash. We just kept explaining what the program was and how it operated (on merit based on tests and interviews) and they didn't like it one bit.

ETHICS AS "APPROPRIATENESS"

The last aspect of the vertical coordinates comes from the language of many global managers that clearly indicates that what they were describing as unethical behavior were differences of considerations of appropriateness or differences of how we view what is appropriate in the world of relationships. Chris Burbach had plenty to say about how she considered some of the treatment of women to be, as she labeled it, unethical in other countries. What disturbed her most was the perception that the women of the country in which she was working were treated quite a bit differently and usually quite poorly in comparison with how she was treated. Chris said:

> As a woman it's a little different, for me. I don't get involved with the heavy drinking and the going out at night, as a lot of my male counterparts do. The result of that is you spend a lot of nights alone in a hotel. I have noticed the difference in how the people that I work with in Asia treat me, versus treating my Asian female colleagues. They're much more inclined to listen to me, and they have more respect for western women.

Chris went on to tell this story:

> I was in Hong Kong meeting with some Hong Kong Chinese about one of our programs. A Hong Kong Chinese woman was to meet me there, along with a woman from the U.K. I came in first, and about 15 minutes later, the Hong Kong Chinese woman came in. She was stopped by guards and assumed to be a prostitute. This woman complained to the manager, and he was apologetic, but it didn't stop him from making some really inappropriate comments. In Korea I've noticed that there is a Korean woman running the office there. They chew her up. The woman just sits there—there are too many cultural mores there for her to do anything about it. She just simply couldn't act as their equal. It's the same in Indonesia.

Chris' anger and discomfort at how these women are treated is understandable. Yet is it really unethical or simply culturally inappropriate, according to our cultural norms about equality?

Joe Villarreal is Network Product Manager in charge of vendor relationship sales for networking and products with Sirius Computers, based in San Antonio, Texas. The vendors with whom Joe works in this capacity are some of the biggest in the country in the high-tech field. They're the Motorolas, the IBMs, the Cisco Computers. Joe is bilingual and bicultural. He grew up in a Hispanic culture on the border of Texas and Mexico and he went to school in the United States. He started working for Sirius Computer Solutions 8 years ago. Soon after he was hired, the Motorola office in Huntsville informed Sirius that Motorola needed someone to distribute their product in Mexico, because an increasing number of clients and cities there were interested in their products. Because Joe was bilingual and understood the culture, he was tapped for the job.

Even for someone who was raised in the Hispanic culture, this was a learning experience, particularly in terms of the importance of language. There were different dialects. According to Joe:

> You can understand the words. But, are they asking or stating an opinion? Little by little I learned how to do things. I'm sure that a lot of the things that Mexicans do in their business interactions are labeled as unethical by their American counterparts; in fact I know they are because they're some of my business colleagues. Mexicans all want to be exclusive, they want to be able to say, I'm the only one who can sell you this, so you have to buy it from me. The fortunes in Mexico are made by individuals who sold things exclusively. Traditionally, this is the way some of our vendors chose to operate in Mexico—with one distributor in one city or one county.
>
> Where we get it wrong as American businessmen is that we go down there and come back. We expect huge deals. We think that we have won the customer, but that only happens after many, many months. We just don't understand the value and the importance of building relationships, that that's what the deal is based on in Mexico. It's not based on a contract—it's based on relationship. Sometimes the path to that relationship, from our North American eyes anyway, seems a little less than straight. Mexico will have a product and they'll say to the customer, here's what you need—and they sell it regardless of what the customer needs. Whereas we look for what the customer wants and then try to sell that. There's a lot of expectation about give and take in the business. The next time your clients will win a big deal for you. That's how they do business and if you're not aware of it, it's your fault. However, other American businessmen experiencing these same kinds of interactions look at them and say that's not right—they're not doing this right. This isn't ethical. They do things down there in the name of business—that just absolutely

drives us crazy—that we label all kinds of things. I would advocate that it is simply understanding that what they are doing is inappropriate in our culture, but not necessarily unethical.

Let me give you an example of a situation I had recently. We get marketing funds from manufacturers. We had funds to provide 3 weeks of engineering training in Mexico City, and it was made very clear to the distributor (from my point of view, anyway) that they could only send *one* person. I only had the funds for each distributor to send *one* person. In just a short while I got a call from the manufacturer saying that I needed another purchase order because the first company had sent two people. I went back to the first company and said, "What are you doing? I very clearly said you could only send one person." His response was to say accusatorily, "You don't want to invest in me."And I yelled back, 'What do you mean I don't want to invest in you? I just gave you $10,000!' He didn't see it. They think we're making 20 percent on every deal because that's how they do it. They're not afraid I'll take away their business. I'm still a foreigner, but I speak their language. They don't like to do business in English. When I meet with them, I tell them I'm not going to participate in anything that's construed as illegal. Now that has a broad interpretation to them—although I must say it's no longer acceptable in Mexico to do many of these things either.

Something else that goes in doing business in Mexico is that this high priority they have on relationship gets carried over to the social aspects of business. From the point of view of many Americans, it goes way above and beyond the normal kinds of business socializing that is standard practice in the U.S. In Mexico, they want to meet you socially first to see if they want to do business. They want to be able to do business with people that they like and that they trust. When this happens to the U.S. salespeople, being invited to the Mexican businessperson's home, being involved with their family, being taken out on the town night after night, the U.S. salesperson becomes uncomfortable. There's another practice of Mexican businessmen which really drives U.S. people crazy and flies straight in the face of our perception of what is appropriate in business, some of the general principles of doing business that we take for granted. They consistently ask for credit and state that, "I'll pay you as soon as my customer pays me." When we tried to help them understand that that's not an acceptable way to do business, they get offended. For them, there's no other way to do business. They'll say, "It's not that I don't want to pay you, but if my customer doesn't pay me, how can I pay you?"

Other Americans get very frustrated and label a lot of things that go on in Mexico as unethical, dishonest. I'll tell my business partners I need something by Friday, and their response is, "No problem." Along comes Friday and there's no document, payment, product, whatever it was that was agreed to. So I call up the customer and I'll say, "Hey, it's Friday. Where is it?" And the person says, "No problem, I'll get it to you by this afternoon." But of course the afternoon comes and goes and the agreement isn't fulfilled. It's not that they're being dishonest, it's that they want to keep you happy. That's the priority. In their culture, if there's an excuse, it's okay. Even an excuse as simple as "I forgot" is okay. These are the kinds of things that get labeled as inappropriate business behavior and even unethical. They're dishonest, they're deceitful. They lie.

Another example of this was a meeting that had been scheduled around a big contract. I asked all the parties that were involved from the Mexico side of the business several times, "Are you going to be there?" "Oh yes, oh yes," they said. Well it comes time for the meeting, and they didn't show up. I was furious. I called them and said, "What happened?" The partner said, "Well, we had some vacations planned and we forgot." We forgot! We forgot! That's enough of an excuse. It's a different mindset about business that we get frustrated and angry towards and then label as unethical, as dishonest, as laziness. In Mexico, the family comes first. Work definitely comes second.

Because Joe Villereal knows and understands the Mexican culture, he experiences these transgressions in a slightly different way. No less frustrated by the inconvenience and the inappropriateness of business partners' saying they will do something and then not doing it, he nontheless understands where the behavior arises from culturally and is less inclined to indict the individual or the entire culture. Instead of damning the behavior as unethical, he can see it as a fundamentally different way of viewing the world and try to plan around it. On Joe's ethical map, the incidents would be within the coordinates of behavior that is seen on the cultural level and deemed unethical because it is inappropriate on one level and violates the U.S. sense of what truthfulness means in business interactions.

As we can see from Joe's experience and the experiences of others navigating the ethical map, these definitions and coordinates do not always put us squarely into one category or quadrant. More often than not, they tend to cluster in certain co-ordinates and can help us get a clearer picture of what is actually happening in any business transaction and why we are having an emotional, powerful, and direct reaction to the situation.

In Chapter 5, we explore the different levels of ethical inter-action to which these different map coordinates lead. We also look at specific actions that indicate when we are engaging at each level and how to move between and among the levels when we desire it or it is required.

Chapter 5

Journeying with Your Ethical Map

"Nothing is so terrifying as a demonstration of principle."
                    ... PAUL GRUCHOW, *OUR SUSTAINABLE TABLE*

In Chapter 4 we looked at a framework for understanding and assessing the different types of behaviors—individual, organizational, and cultural or global—in which people engage and which are labeled to one degree or another as unethical. We looked at breaking down the overall map of ethics according to whether something is clearly corrupt, fraudulent, or illegal; unethical according to our cultural and personal values; unfair according to our capitalistic political mindset; or inappropriate according to our personal cultural behavioral standards. We looked at categories of behavior through the lenses of the individual, the organization, and the culture of the global organization as a whole. This chapter will focus again on specific behaviors using the lenses of the individual, the organization, and the global or cultural aspect. We look at the different levels of coping and dealing with ethical issues according to three levels, levels that I call Survival, Understanding, and Knowing. Each of these levels has a different task or purpose, a specific focus of engagement, and a particular challenge through which leaders must work. The first level is Survival.

Survival issues for an individual, an organization, or a culture revolve around behaviors that help us simply to exist, to go unnoticed and not stand out in another culture in any way. Survival behaviors allow us to engage at the minimal level of behavior and engagement with another individual, organization, or culture without committing any faux pas or mistakes that make us stand out in a way for which we would be considered inadequate, inappropriate, or ineffective. Survival behaviors for an individual, an organization, or a culture are primarily concerned with remaining intact.

The next level of complexity in journeying with an ethical map for an individual, organization, or culture, is the level that I call *Understanding*. At the level of understanding, you and I are both working through the lenses of our own cultures and ethical values. The emphasis, however, is on two-way communication and an acknowledgment that there are at least two parties in the transaction

Survival

Task: Remain Intact
Do Not Stand Out

Focus: On Oneself

Challenge: Understanding Who I Am in
Another Cultural

Figure 5.1 The level of ethical survival behaviors for an individual, an organization, or a culture are primarily concerned with remaining intact.

whose interests, values, and requirements must be taken into consideration. Understanding increases our knowledge of ourselves by providing a point of contact against which our own behaviors and attitudes are reflected back to us. Understanding provides information about The Other (Said 1991). When we choose to journey with our ethical map on the level of Understanding, we choose to consider the other person's context, knowledge, and information with how we behave. It's a two-way street, a double-loop transaction in which by understanding each other, we change our understanding about each other (Argyris and Schon 1974).

The third level of complexity to explore in journeying with the ethical map is the level of *Knowing*. When we choose to engage on the level of Knowing, the information about ourselves and the information and knowledge that we gain through an interaction of the whole—the whole person, the whole culture, the whole spirit of another—creates a level of knowledge greater than that contained by the components in each of them (Kegan 1995). In fact, the process of Knowing creates entirely new knowledge about both of us that was previously not available to either of us.

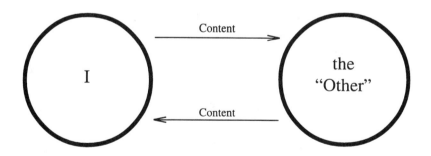

Task: Two-Way Engagement

Focus: Mutual Understanding of the "Other"

Challenge: Simultaneously Understanding and Respecting Two Points of View

Figure 5.2 The level of ethical understanding includes others and their points of view.

"DON'T TIP THE SCANDINAVIAN CAB DRIVERS!": INDIVIDUAL SURVIVAL

Let's look now at what journeying with your map on each of these levels can mean for your experience in engaging in another culture around a business issue.

In the summer of 1981, I began working for the Global Shipping Division of the Chase Manhattan Bank. The global shipping division was the corporate banking department that provided financing for vessel owners and operators around the world. My job was newly created at a time when banks were just beginning to realize that they needed to learn how to market their products and services in addition to the traditional lending operations that had been the mainstay of the banking industry for thousands of years. As the Global Operations Marketing Manager, my staff and I were responsible for the research, design, development, implementation, and marketing of what we called non-loan products. For the Global Shipping Division's customers, these products were used in international trade, such as letters of credit, special bill-payment collection systems for liner companies, special international money transfer arrangements—basically anything that was not a loan. Within 2 weeks of starting my new assignment at the bank, I was sent on a 3-week business trip to meet with our shipping customers in key locations. The purpose of the trip was to learn more about the operational side of customers' businesses in order to design and develop operational products. On this trip I was scheduled to be in six countries in only a few weeks.

When the day arrived for my departure on this eagerly awaited business excursion, I walked out of my office to catch the elevator to the street level of the office building to find a taxi to the airport. I waddled out of the office carrying a huge, overstuffed shoulder garment bag, a very large carry-on bag, a large camera bag complete with telephoto and panoramic lenses, a briefcase stuffed to capacity, a large handbag, and a shopping bag filled with small tokens for the international hosts with whom I would be meeting and working. As I struggled out to the elevator and pushed the down button my boss, the global division executive, leaned his head into the hallway and yelled, "Don't tip the Scandinavian cab drivers!" It was the only piece of cross-cultural business advice I was to receive before, during, or after this business trip. At the time I was completely mystified as to what it was supposed to mean.

What I've learned over the years working internationally and working with many individual managers, both home and abroad as well as those who work in virtual organizations in which the globe is the office is that very few people receive any kind of useful preparation at all. Typically what happens is that individuals find their own sources of information and support for doing business in another country. We load ourselves down with travel guides (along with our luggage and cameras). We might even check a videotape out of the local library. We can now look up many sites on the Internet that deal with a particular country or region. Survival information typically is covered in a course, book, or article on the "Dos and Don'ts of Doing Business In…." Not to be discounted by any means, these kinds of resources, which are becoming more available in bookstores and to individual travelers, are useful, practical, and in a very basic sense of the words, life savers.

More progressive organizations have for years been offering some form of rudimentary language training for a particular region. Back in the days when the only type of international or global exposure was an overseas assignment as an expatriate, this information was particularly useful. If I am being sent to Jakarta for 5 years to run the technology division there, then knowing the ins and outs of everyday life in Indonesia will be useful, and I will be given a small gift of time to actually learn what I eventually need to know. In today's global environment, however, a sales manager or a field engineer can be in Dubai one day, Berlin another day, and end up the week in Hong Kong. Even if there was time to learn the language in all these locations, it wouldn't be feasible. The problem with this kind of survival training for individuals working in the global environment is that facts and figures don't address what is fundamentally at stake in this kind of a situation.

Mike Morgan, senior engineer at Conoco, has spent his entire career at Conoco and has been assigned as engineering project manager on multimillion dollar natural gas projects around the world, from Dubai to Norway, Trinidad to New Mexico. Says Mike:

> The problems are not in the megadeal, like airplanes to Saudi Arabia. The problem is pretty penny ante, until the stakes get too high. At some point you have to put a stake in the ground that you're not in that kind of business. The problem is you feel alone and isolated and you lose proper perspective of what is happening. You feel like you're the only one involved in a situation that you've been approached about and you think, "If I tell anybody, I'll get in trouble and then I'll just have to run off—I can't possibly face the organization."

It's this sense of isolation, of aloneness, of not knowing where to turn, that the survival books do not address. The dos and don'ts of a culture—"Don't show the bottom of your shoe to Arabs"—don't begin to address the sense of loneliness and isolation that a new manager or a young manager feels in this kind of situation. "Don't tip the Scandinavian cab drivers" is useful advice for making sure you aren't cheated during the drive from the airport to the city center, but it doesn't quell the sense of disease, of feeling alone in an unfamiliar situation in which you feel there are no clear boundaries. Survival has different faces, and we as individuals and the organizations in which we work have tended to look at only one. In addition to questions of physical survival—How do I dress? Can I figure out the money? Should I bow or shake hands? How do I get from the airport to the hotel?—there are questions of psychological and personal survival—How will I deal with my feelings of aloneness? Will I know what to do if I have a real problem? Can I be myself in a business situation?

One of the interesting things I learned in my conversations with managers at all levels in organizations, on issues of ethics in cross-cultural situations is that the higher up in an organization a person is, the more he or she takes for granted that appropriate ethical structures are in place and that people know the right things to do. Senior managers appear to operate with a sense that everyone knows that ethical behavior is important and that individuals are driven by the right values. There is more of a sense of dis-ease among managers and individual contributors who directly touch the operations of the business or who are in the field as opposed to a headquarters or corporate location. This dichotomy became clear to me when I was teaching management and leadership development programs at large corporate universities across the United States. On one memorable occasion, a morning session included a 1-hour lecture from the chief legal counsel of the organization in which he went through the legal vulnerabilities of the organization when managers violate in any way the Foreign Corrupt Practices Act. The legal counsel discussed the items point by point: giving and receiving gifts, conflicts of interest, and all the way down the line. Back in the classroom and in small groups, the managers erupted into an intense and emotional discussion about "how it really is." It was dramatic in its intensity and poignant in its pain as very good human beings conveyed in detail what it is like to confront these issues on a daily basis. These were all managers or individuals who led teams. They were not the most senior cut of the organization, but they were all at a high mid-manager level

An individual's quest for survival is a lonely journey in which data is sought in the absence of self-confidence or experience, in which structure is created in the absence of clear requirements, and in which the minutiae of cultural idiosyncrasies are memorized and sought in the absence of any intuitive or meaningful understanding of cultural process.

Organizations also focus most of their attention on this aspect of survival. It is here on the map that we find growing attention paid to ethics codes, ethics officers, ethics training, and other formulaic aspects of business and ethics in global companies. In 1994, the Ethics Resource Center, based in Washington, D.C., conducted a comprehensive survey among organizations and how they provide ethical training, ethics codes, and other ethical support. The center found that a growing number of companies have ethics programs. Sixty percent of respondents reported that their companies had a code of conduct. (Other surveys, such as that of the Conference Board have reported higher incidences.) Thirty-three percent of respondents reported that their company had training on business and ethics and 33% reported that their companies had an ethics ombudsman (Ethics Resource Center 1994).

These ethics codes and training programs are no doubt a direct result of survival of another sort. In 1991 the U.S. government enacted Sentencing Guidelines for companies convicted of ethical violations. For companies that demonstrate evidence of formal ethical policies, the penalties incurred are drastically reduced. It would be easy to take the cynic's view and declare that companies go through the effort of developing ethical codes only to avoid the harsher sentencing penalties or that ethics training in companies is merely window dressing for what "everybody knows" is just "common sense."

Dismissing things as common sense is the way out for the person too lazy to do the thinking required. In spite of the potential for cynicism, these codes, and the internal organizational processes that lead to them, very often have positive results. One of the findings of the Ethics Resource Center survey was that employees generally found ethics programs valuable in guiding their decision making and conduct. The employees, however, also generally preferred to follow the chain of command and turn to their direct supervisor for advice about ethical issues.

Figure 5.3 Dilbert 5/30/95 reprinted by permission of United Feature Syndicate, Inc.

MOVING FROM SURVIVING TO UNDERSTANDING

Just as one would assume, when journeying on the map as an individual, managers are concerned about survival, about themselves individually, about making sure they don't do anything to embarrass themselves or the company. Managers want to know they can get their basic day-to-day personal and business needs met. In moving to understanding, the scope broadens so that managers are concerned about and take into account information about the other organization, the other individual, and the other culture.

Just as language and the acquisition of basic language skills can be a survival tactic for an individual, they can be a means of moving from survival to understanding in another culture, because language and culture are inseparable. Remember the story of Joe Villereal, the product network manager who was bicultural and bilingual:

> Even though I spoke the language, it was a learning experience for me in terms of the language. There are different dialects. You could understand the words, but are they asking questions? Are they stating an opinion? Little by little, I learned how to do things through getting around with the language. There are some subtleties in the language that knowing the language helps enormously in understanding that culture, in dealing with that culture.

Understanding how language is used in other cultures can be helpful in navigating ethical situations. For instance, it is still customary for most business transactions and social transactions in Russia to be conducted by the business partners in Russian using translators. This is in keeping with policies and practices in the Russian culture that appear to give the Russians an advantage. Just knowing about that particular business and cultural process, however, and having that bit of understanding about the culture can help individual managers be more prepared in acquiring their own translators or in negotiating the use of translators ahead of time.

Understanding a Culture

When individual managers in a cross-cultural situation have a greater understanding of the individual and his or her culture, they have more options for making decisions and more options for behaving.

Survival: Organizational

The next stop on our journey with our ethical map is to look at what organizations do to survive in cross-cultural dilemmas. This place on the map is where the organizational policies, ethics codes, and training programs are found in great abundance. In 1994, the Ethics Resource Center, based in Washington, DC, conducted a comprehensive survey among organizations about how they provide ethics training, ethics codes, and other organizational support. An increasing number of organizations already have ethics codes. Whether these codes are developed as a proactive statement to employees and the public about who they wish to be in the world or the codes are developed as defensive actions against severe penalties in line with the 1991 Sentencing Guidelines, we cannot truly say. Many are plaques on the wall. Others are true articulations of a company's hope for how it wants to be in the world.

Even companies that have developed ethics codes and policies have done so mostly with their eyes inward into their own organizations. Most company ethics policies, codes, training, and officers are designed for and used primarily for decision making within the company itself and among its employees. This tends to become cloudier in a cross-cultural context in that ethical decision making outside the U.S. and outside domestic U.S. companies tend to involve issues around decision makers or factors outside the company itself. For instance, in the Ethics Resource Center survey, the behavior that appeared to be the most common type of ethical misconduct observed by employees was lying. Most of the respondents who observed misconduct had witnessed lying to supervisors (56 percent) and other employees' lying on reports or falsifying records (41 percent). One third of respondents who had witnessed misconduct, said it was around sexual harassment, stealing, drug or alcohol abuse, and conflicts of interest. These are all ethical problems that are being observed by one employee and within one company. Specific ethics codes and policies appear to be more useful in a United States–based situation and tend to provide more guidance and assistance at home. Once outside the United States reliance seems to be strongly on the Foreign Corrupt Practices Act, which specifies behaviors considered unethical. These are boundaries set from outside the limits of the organization itself and one of the reasons there is a gap in organizational support for transactions made outside the United States. Organizations go to another level of complexity when they try to make suppliers adhere to the same ethical values and standards they require of each other internally.

Scott Thomas, vice president of sourcing for Reebok, highlighted this phenomenon when he described his relationships with supplier factories. Reebok does not own or manage the resources directly, yet because it works on basically a sole-supplier basis, the company does strongly influence the day-to-day operations of the factories and hold them to a standard different from the ones the factory would hold for itself.

Organizational Practices in Ethics Training

The practices around ethics policies and training in the companies in which I spoke to individuals were remarkably similar. Alain Batty, executive director for Asia Pacific and new markets development of Ford Motor Company, referred to a standard letter issued around September. He said he knows of issues of ethical violations in India and China but he is not directly confronted with them. "Our people," he said, however, "are very, very aware of ethical issues. But I'm not concerned about it at all. It's not new, it's a very strong policy. The first letter I signed was a letter about our ethical policies. Integrity," he goes on, "comes up in the mission–guiding principles and speeches around that. No one could not know what our organizational policy is around ethics. There's absolutely no flexibility. It's not about money or dollars. It's about infringing rules."

Mr. Batty's colleague at Ford, Richard Beattie, the sales and marketing executive for Latin America, Canada, and Mexico, supported Batty's statement.

> We sign a C-103 document. It's a very comprehensive document. The higher up you go, the more important it is that you sign. It covers the dos and don'ts of relationships with suppliers and becomes a part of your contract of employment. It's been in place for about 15 years or so.

John Klein of Union Texas Petroleum stated:

> Our main guidelines stray from the ethical realm more into the legal. You sign something that says you will adhere to the FCPA [Foreign Corrupt Practices Act]. In terms of ethical behavior, the company has formal values and mission statements. They just say, "We are an ethical company," but that's all. It's unwritten and unsaid about how you are to behave in and out of the office when you're representing Union Texas. There's a certain way to behave, and it's unspoken. But you know when you're straying from it.

States Mike Morgan:

> At Conoco you're shown a video on FCPA and threatened with a battery of lawyers. As far as training on our ethical policy goes we have confidential hotlines for other things, like drug abuse and whistle blowing, and there are legal references in the back of our phone books, but it's mostly the video that people are counting on to communicate the ethical policies.

Richard Beattie says much the same about Ford:

> Videotapes give people examples, such as suppliers and advertising relationships. There are guidelines for when to take advantage of that. Ford has been a finance-driven company—the policies you see are financially driven. Whenever there have been a few examples of people who have strayed over the boundary in

the company, you suddenly see a flurry of videos in every department. If people are working in an environment that promotes more "creativity" you show them the way through [potential dilemmas] by key policies and benefits.

Citibank has a slightly different approach, according to Devin Archer:

> There is ethics training, but it's not something that you start with when you join the company or that you go through automatically. It's more for high-level management, when you're going to be leading people. It's more like a train the trainer—they don't do it for everyone—they just train the supervisors and the leaders and the others who then cascade it down through the organization.

When General Electric launched its integrity program it also launched a 2-hour training program for everyone in the company, worldwide.

One of the problems with the new trend toward developing codes of ethics and ethics policies is that in some instances they have become an end in themselves. For many companies these codes and policies have become showpieces that look good to the public, look good to the stockholder, and certainly look good to the government should the company get in trouble with sentencing guidelines around ethical violations. But to many managers these codes are little more than a plaque on the wall. Joseph L. Badaracco, Jr. mentions as much in his book, *Defining Moments,* as does Thomas Donaldson, one of the leading academic researchers on business and ethics and the director of the ethics program at Wharton's School of Business. Donaldson calls it "company code plastering, pasting them on the wall."

More companies are establishing a position of ethics officer in their companies as another way to survive the journey through business and ethics. In Waltham, Massachusetts, the Ethics Officers Association is part of the Center for Business and Ethics housed within the Bentley College business program. The Ethics Officers Association has experienced considerable growth recently and now runs full-fledged certification programs for ethics officers and has in the undergraduate business ethics program an entire curriculum relating to the functions of ethics.

Another indication that ethics policies and ethics codes are sources of pride and public relations for many companies is that many company ethics codes can be found on the Internet as examples of good practices. More books are being published than ever before, such as Allen Reeder's *75 Best Business Practices for Socially Responsible Companies,* and Patricia Jones and Larry Kahaner's *Say It and Live It: The Fifty Corporate Mission Statements That Hit the Mark.* These are examples of how the existence of an ethics policy can be good public relations for a company as well as practical guidance. However, in moving from survival to understanding in a journey with your ethical map, something has to happen beyond hanging a plaque on the wall.

One of my favorite stories is the story about Potemkin Village. Although there is some debate about whether the story is historical or apocryphal, the metaphor is still a good one to apply to the subject of organizations and ethics codes. Grigory Aleksandro-vich Potemkin, born in 1739, was a Russian army officer and statesman. For 17 years he was the most powerful man in Russia. For 2 years he was also the lover of Empress Catherine II. He helped bring Catherine to power as empress, and in 1774 she made him commander-in-chief and governor general of New Russia. Potemkin became field marshal in 1784 and introduced many reforms to the army. He also had a penchant for doing things on a grand scale: the arsenal of Kherson was begun in 1778, the harbor of Sevastopol was built in 1784, and a new fleet of 15 ships and 25 smaller vessels were built in the Black Sea. These projects, along with Potemkin's attempts to colonize the Ukrainian steppes, were miscalculated in terms of cost, and his grand designs had to be abandoned though half built. In 1787 Catherine began a train tour of the south to witness the great advances and accomplishments. Potemkin managed to camouflage all of his weaknesses, as the tale goes, by erecting artificial villages—storefronts and false facades—that could be seen by the Empress as her train passed through the villages, hiding the half-built and decrepit structures of the real village. *Potemkin village* has come to stand for any undesirable or incomplete condition that is covered up by a well-crafted or pretentious façade. At worst, ethics codes are the Potemkin village of business ethics, well crafted, glossily published, and presented with color and flourish. At best they are what they say they are: meaningful guideposts for managers. When moving from survival to understanding, the question we must ask is: What would it take to make a Potemkin village of organizational ethics codes into a real city?

How Organizations Move Toward Understanding

The first step that is absolutely essential for a company moving from "Survival" to "Understanding" is acknowledging the corporate values upon which the company will stand in the marketplace. This is the first and fundamental block in building organizational understanding around ethical codes in global organizations. Who are we? For what do we want to be known? How do we want to be remembered? To do that, what are some of the policies we want to put into place? How will we behave with each other here at home and with our customers, clients, vendors, and partners abroad? What does it take for real and useful understanding to occur in an organization that is journeying with an ethical map?

Richard Beattie, of Ford, states:

> We think a lot about this as we are engaged in our Ford 2000 process. Things are tougher globally. We're working with the attributes around leadership and what that really means to us in being a global company. There's a quality of judgment that's here—that we have to rely on peoples' judgments and let them get on with it. There's also a growing awareness that we need to be much, much more open about backgrounds, cultures, sexual orientation. We have to demonstrate that we're open to that in order to effectively act ethically around the world. We have people coming to Detroit and presenting more complex issues. They're coming from Vietnam, Thailand, India, China, Singapore. The other awareness that we've come to is that a way of doing business has to reflect the management with the people from the backgrounds and the countries with whom we do business. We

can't just continue to be a bunch of U.S. managers sitting in Detroit and hoping that we will be effective outside of Detroit.

This is a good example of an organization coming to grips with what it needs to know and understand about itself to be effective globally.

Devon Archer , of Citibank, had this to say about the role of moving from Survival to Understanding in an organization:

Ethical codes are hard to define. The people here in Vietnam have suffered. They've been shut out from the world for too long. For too long, people have been told half truths. Here there's no such thing as a handshake deal. Prior to talking there's what they call a "Memorandum of Understanding." In the States, something like this wouldn't hold water. They base a lot of deals on sensitive understandings. But over here, because of their history, because of who they have been and what they know and their role in the world, we need to approach them with more understanding of who we're dealing with. For instance, that Memorandum of Understanding or an MOU, as we call them over here, is established for every meeting that you go into. It's a Memorandum of Understanding that we're going to talk about these following things. In the U.S. you talk about something, you go to a meeting. They have to overly formalize something that seems insignificant to us, but we need to understand why that's important to them. Not only in terms of being sensitive to the cultures that we're working in but also in order to understand the cultures that we're dealing in so that when it comes time for decisions, we can make the best prepared decision.

Says Mike Morgan, of Conoco:

Training around ethics has to take place on a much different level in the organization when it comes to being effective with business and ethics in global companies. Training—more than just a 2-hour lecture, or handing somebody a notebook, or showing them a video—has got to be more along the lines of sage advice that lets young managers or managers new to the region know, "Here's what can happen." If you do this in a formal indoctrination, it might not be as meaningful. Beyond the technical aspects of a policy code or the Foreign Corrupt Practices Act, we need to have some understanding. This only comes from talking with each other at all levels. This is bigger than just the financial end. What we bring to the situation around safety and environment and treatment of people and technical standards is all of ourselves, everyday.

The human resources consultant from the international oil company picks up this theme as well when she describes the new work environment and how it affects business and ethics in other cultures:

> With all the shift in management over the last decade, with companies restructuring, with companies merging, with people leaving the company and particularly with the senior people leaving the company, there's an issue of continuity. There's a loss of continuity on these issues. Lots of experience is walking out the door—either because it's experience and it's time to leave or they have no choice.

Rebuilding Potemkin

So what can an organization do intentionally to build and foster a relationship of understanding in an organization that moves the organization from the survival mode to understanding mode?

Open lines for dialogue must exist above and beyond the traditional chain of command. Managers must create an atmosphere in which people feel free to talk about ethical issues without fear of retribution, without fear of looking disloyal, and without fear of looking ignorant of the company codes. A practical system of one-on-one mentoring is critical. Experienced managers must take younger and new managers directly under their wings.

Make contracts about specific ways that you as a manager will be there to answer specific questions and to mull over some of the difficult experiences that others might be having. Find a way, on an individual basis or through small-group dialogue, before a colleague begins to deal with another culture to help that person understand the philosophy, the intent, and the corporate culture of the other and prepare him or her to deal with that. The most effective way to do this is through mentoring.

MOVING FROM UNDERSTANDING TO KNOWING

What does it take to move from rebuilding a Potemkin village to thriving in a real city? The symbol that represents Knowing in an organization about cross-cultural business ethics is in Figure 5.4.

At this level, the task of knowing becomes that of creating new knowledge together. It is different from understanding in that I am moving beyond what I know and understanding what you know to that of mutually creating something that did not exist before. When we are operating at the level of Knowing, we are focusing on the meaning behind our actions and what it creates for us. The only way we can arrive at the level of Knowing is by staying in a place of dialogue in which we must hold opposing truths at the same time. Ethical knowing is not cultural relativism in which we accept all actions in the name of openness. It is often an intuitive level of ethical knowing that occurs over a period of time when we are in a relationship with the others with whom we are working. It is knowledge that allows us as managers to make the leap across the chasm between organizational policies and what is effective in communicating the ethics of a company.

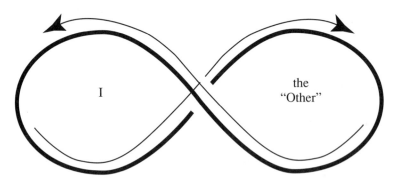

Task: Knowing-Creating Knowledge Together that is More Than What We Know Individually

Focus: Meaning

Challenge: Holding Two Opposing Points of View at the Same Time ("and" not either/or thinking & interactions)

Figure 5.4 The Level of Ethical Knowing

This concept of Ethical Knowing is illustrated by the work of Dr. Lynn Richards and what she calls Relational Knowledge (Richards 1998). In relational knowledge, our knowledge comes through deep interaction rather than interpretation from someone else or through data and analysis. The point of focus is collective rather than individual or in parallel with another. The evidence that we have such knowledge is the evidence of trust between us and the other. Chapter 6 provides specific examples of how leaders can build trust as part of building ethical competence in an organization.

There is an inherent tension at work in every manager navigating cross-cultural ethical situations. On one side are the knowns—the facts and the expectations. These are the "hard" elements of ethical behavior. On the other side is the completely subjective evaluation of the situation—the context, the relationships, the specific situation. These are the "soft" elements of ethical behavior. Organizations must provide the hard elements and empower managers to make ethical judgments and choices on the soft elements. The organization must provide structure and clear boundaries. There must also be flexibility and trust on the part of the company to allow managers to navigate successfully. "No one in our company has ever tried to second guess my actions on behalf of safety—in this country or any country," states Michael Morgan, of Conoco.

Norb Roobaert, president and chief executive officer of Alliance Engineering, told me about much of the work he had done in collaborations with managers and organizations in Russia and China.

> This issue of trust and how it gets played out between cultures was such an eye opener for us when my counterpart in the Russian design company and I gave a joint presentation at the Society of Petroleum Engineers. We gave equal time to both sides of the process, in terms of what Americans think about working with Russians and what Russians think about working with Americans.
>
> The room was absolutely packed, and I'm convinced they weren't there to hear what I had to say about the Russians. We

learned over the course of this collaboration that trust can look quite different from one culture to another. It was in the working together and truly listening to each and learning to respect each other's knowledge, ideas, and values that we were able to create something between our two companies that was effective, that was profitable, and from both of our perspectives was ethical.

What Organizations Can Do to Move from Understanding to Knowing

CROSS-BUSINESS DIALOGUES: Using Live Cases to Understand Business and Ethics Cross Culturally

In the early 1990s, the General Electric Company's Leadership Development Institute, informally known as Crotonville, developed a learning process known as *the live case*. Instead of relying on well-crafted businesses cases from the Harvard Business School or the host of other sources that provide such cases, GE chose to bring in participants who were involved in actual change efforts in an organization. They discussed decisions that had to be made and things that had to be changed. Through a structured process of introducing the issues to the company or class, setting up questions, and providing a model for learning those issues, the live case has become institutionalized as a vibrant, effective, and relevant way to learn. In the summer of 1997, I led a week-long business and ethics forum at the Chautauqua Institution, the oldest adult education institution in the United States, founded in 1898, on issues of business and ethics. Drawing on four different companies, we orchestrated live cases in which the actual players in a company that had been involved in ethical decision making presented the various sides of the issue. The group participants—using a model—not only reached their own conclusions but also initiated a dialogue with the actual players regarding their thinking and their decisions. Just as at General Electric, the participants at The Chautauqua Institution Forum came away with greater awareness of the complexities of the issues and certainly a greater understanding of many sides of the issues.

One very practical intervention organizations can sponsor and initiate to move from understanding to knowing in this critical dimension of organizational life is to structure live cases around ethical decision-point dilemmas, a fuzziness that actual managers experience. We have learned to look at our dilemmas in business and ethics as binary, either-or choices. We typically start with a cultural stereotype, factor in a well-intentioned and crafted policy, isolate ourselves with our questions or yearning for dialogue, and proceed. On the other hand, we continue to agonize sometimes over small transactions that we feel may adversely affect our business relationships. We never fully understand that standing firm, working with utter conviction, communicating with clarity, and building a legacy of becoming a known quantity will serve us well and more easily than we could have imagined. We are not consigned to simple survival in our ethical behaviors. We have a choice—and most certainly the means—to move from Surviving through Understanding and into knowing. There are many managers who want to do the right thing. We need to raise the banner and let others know we are out there. We do not have to travel alone.

Chapter 6

Charting the Course Through Leadership

"Even if you're on the right track, you'll get run over if you just sit there."
                                                    . . . WILL ROGERS

"I find the great thing in this world is not so much where we stand as in what direction we are moving. To reach the port of heaven, we must sail sometimes with the wind and sometimes against it—but we must sail, and not drift, nor lie at anchor."
                                        . . . OLIVER WENDELL HOLMES

"Relationships are like sharks. They have to keep moving all the time or they die. What we have here is a dead shark."
                                . . . WOODY ALLEN, FROM *ANNIE HALL*

In the previous chapters several important themes have emerged: (1) We can no longer hide behind confusion or plead ignorance, attempt to "research later," or throw up our hands in despair about how to make ethical decisions in global companies. (2) Because shifting global economic foundations have

133

resulted in increased global interactions and transactions, organizations have responded with downsizing, outsourcing, and spreading their human resources thinner and thinner in the name of global competitiveness. (3) We must start making ethical decisions and understanding global partners in a broader perspective, use more precise language, and use an ethical map to understand where our personal and organizational dilemmas lie. (4) We must understand that our ethical actions and our perceptions of others' ethical actions are the result of a system of historical, economic, social, cultural, and individual dynamics, all interacting together in a system of business and ethics and each affecting the other. (5) We move through a process of ethical interaction from Surviving through Understanding to Knowing.

In this chapter I'll share what leaders and managers have shared with me about how to move yourself and your organization through these ethical waters with confidence and caring. You'll hear some final stories from global managers about what really counts in navigating these dilemmas.

THE FOUR ELEMENTS FOR BUILDING ETHICAL COMPETENCE

Even though individuals and organizations tend to focus on one or two of the following key ingredients, all four are critical for building a system that develops ethical competence in organizations.

Discovering and Claiming Your Organizational Values

Meg Hartzler is a partner in the organizational consulting firm Destra, based in Boulder, Colorado. For several years she has helped companies do the difficult work of articulating their values. "One of the things that make this work so challenging," Meg reflected, "is that it takes both left-brained descriptiveness and discipline and right-brained reflectiveness." Meg recently worked with the Asian division of a global pharmaceutical firm to help them create common values for the region despite their very different cultures:

> In the beginning of that project the leadership thought, "We have to tell our people what these values are and what they look like." It wasn't until we had some very powerful sessions of dialogue together, struggling together with the issues, that we began to create and discover our values together. We knew we had to make those values operational, define them in ways that people could translate into what they do and say into their everyday behavior. To do that we used a bulls-eye type chart where values were identified on the outer circle and descriptors or actions were identified on the inside circle.

The common cynical wisdom is that mission, vision, values statements from companies all look the same. One consultant colleague of mine regularly uses an exercise with groups of senior leaders in which he asks them to bring copies of their mission statements, whites out the name of the company, and then flashes them on an overhead screen, asking the individuals to identify their own statements. The embarrassed leaders usually cannot tell the difference from one to the other because so much of the language is interchangeable. So if the actual results of these values exercises seem to produce such common results, why go through the exercise? Where is the value? "When the Asia division was going through this process," replies Meg Hartzler, "we got to a point where we seemed deadlocked, the values seemed to contradict. They'd ask, 'How can we be true to this one and true to that one?' They were looking at each one as if each was in a vacuum."

In values work, descriptors move toward complexity and then to the synergy between them. Our traditional western either-or thinking patterns do not work. We must hold both parts of the paradox simultaneously to hold the context of dialogue. Michael Basseches, the Harvard adult development psychologist, calls it *dialectical thinking*. Robert Kegan calls it feeling as if we are always "in over our heads." Mark Twain said, "The sign of an intelligent person is being able to hold two opposing ideas in your head at

Leadership Behaviors that
Build Ethical Competence

Content	Process	
	"Telling"	"Co-Creating"
1. Leadership Communication	• Memos • Speeches • Annual Reports • Other Documents	• Dialogue about What Ethical Leadership Looks Like/What's Helpful or Useful? • Mentoring One-on-One • Leadership by Being Present
2. Developing Systems for Screening Employees	• Clear Policies • Training for Good Interviewing Skills • Checking References • Good Human Resources Recruitment Practices	• Creating Together Who We Want to Be with Each Other
3. Articulating Values/ Developing Code of Ethics	• Here's What They Are	• Let's Explore and Develop Together
4. Developing & Implementing Ethics Training	• Classroom • Technical or Legal Training	• Action Learning Teams • Live Cross-Cultural Case Studies • Cross-Cultural Dialogues
5. Ensuring that Organizational Systems & Structures Are in Place	• Fraud Detection Processes in Place • Intensive Auditing Processes • Public Punishment Systems • Including in Performance Evaluations • Incorporating Measurement Systems to Measure Identified Aspects	• Building a Community of Ethical Practices throughout the Company • Building a Heritage of Ethics

Figure 6.1 The Components of Ethical Leadership

the same time." To all of us it is the familiar and uncomfortable space of trying to make information into some sort of useful pattern so that we can deal with it, get some distance from it, analyze it, and judge it. Dialectical thinking forces us to deal with the continuing presence of not opposites but of equal truths. It is the hard work of an individual and organization's soul, and most of us would rather not do it. Yet organizations and their leaders who want to develop ethical competence in the global marketplace must do it. Values work, and especially values work that is done well and with integrity, is considered a given in this constellation of elements required for ethical competence.

Having Clear Ethical Codes and Policies

As mentioned in Chapter 5, much energy is being put into developing corporate ethics codes and codes of conduct. The companies that are getting it right are those that build their ethics codes and organizational policies directly on the values they have collectively identified. When ethics codes are written in a conference room by a group of human resources professionals, dictated by the legal department, or handed down by the chief executive officer, without discussion, dialogue, input, and feedback from the larger organization, they tend to invite the kind of skeptical reaction that was found in the 1998 survey of the work of many cartoonists, a joint business school study from Pennsylvania State University and the University of Delaware, released January 9, 1998, and cited in *Business Ethics*, Mar-April 1998. It is frequently a case of "just do as I say, not as I do." The "do as I say" component, however, is still one of the vital ingredients that must be in place. It is important to have the words to craft the policies.

The experience of Cummins Engine with crafting its ethics code gives us an interesting twist on the importance of the element of building ethical competence. Originally a large family owned manufacturing business, the company has Midwest roots and values that have served it well over the almost 100 years it has been in business. Headquartered in the heart of small-town America, Columbus, Indiana, employees have always considered their strong sense of ethical behavior their hallmark, and they are genuinely proud of it. Over the past few decades, Cummins has become increasingly global in suppliers, manufacturing plants, and markets. Along with globalization, has come an increasing number of situations that often run counter to the values and beliefs on which the company was founded. Managers find themselves in situations in which their own sense of personal values derived from deeply embedded American values conflicts with the day-to-day values of relationships and doing business in other cultures.

Only a few years ago the Cummins leadership decided it was time to actually sit down and craft in writing a code of ethics or conduct that could be made clear to all employees and be helpful to the increasing number of managers dealing with complex cross-cultural situations. Amazingly, in this company utterly devoted to ethical behavior, there was enormous pushback from employees at all levels. It would be an insult to who we are and who we understand each other to be, they declared, to have to put those principles into writing.

Communication of Organizational Values, Ethics Codes, and Personal Expectations

The third component for building ethical competence in organizations is how policies are communicated throughout the organization. There are now some specific best practices we can draw from companies who are Getting It Right.

Codes must be written and made accessible in as many ways as possible. Mary Ann Pearce, vice president of Conoco International Natural Gas, a subsidiary of Conoco, tells how Conoco communicates is ethical policies and code:

> It's all over a lot of our documents. It's in the statements in the annual reports. We sign a compliance form every year. Our executives talk about our values all the time. We have a strict termination policy if there is abuse of expense accounts or any other kind of perceived ethical violation. This is a pretty small company, so everyone knows why so-and-so was terminated. It's talked about publicly, as well as around the water cooler.

Some companies also engage in ethics training in which employees are presented with the ethics policies and codes. In most companies these sessions, usually 1 to 2 hours, are presented by members of the human resources department or, more likely, the legal department. Devon Archer, of Citibank Vietnam, said that supervisors at certain levels attend the training and then they are expected to pass it down to their employees. At best this seems to be a hit-and-miss process.

A few companies spoke about informal one-to-one mentoring of younger employees or employees new to the company or new to a geographic region to prepare them for cross-cultural situations that can pose dilemmas or anxiety. For managers who have been the recipient of this kind of personal tutelage, it clearly has had a powerful effect on them and was of tremendous help. I have not come across any kind of institutionalized mentoring system, however, even though several managers have suggested it.

A fourth kind of best practice that I have come across is the live case—a process that brings together all the players, or representatives of the players, in a cross-cultural issue to dialogue (through a specific process) about the issue at hand by the parties involved. This type of communication is in the category of dialectical dialogue and results in a higher order of knowledge for everyone involved. This is the type of knowledge that results when all the elements of the ethical system interact, as discussed in Chapter 5.

Leadership

Clearly the thing that matters most to individuals navigating cross-cultural ethics is the component of leadership. It is also the component that matters most in building ethical competence in an organization. It is the component with quantum leverage on each of the other three components for developing a system of organizational ethical competence. Luckily, the stories from many managers give us the ability to define ethical leadership as more than the usual "You'll know it when you see it."

What Does Ethical Leadership Look Like?

Dave Ulrich, author, consultant, and faculty member at the University of Michigan Business School says there are three simple, clear indicators for whether a leader is providing leadership in a certain strategic area, as follows:

1. How do you spend your time? Do you pass what Ulrich calls the calendar test? Does your personal planner have time blocked out or appointments made to discuss this issue? How much time are you spending on the subject of ethics in your global company? Ten minutes a year? Ten minutes a quarter? Ten minutes a day?

2. What degree of passion and focus do you have for the topic of ethical behavior? If you were arrested for focusing on ethical behavior in your company, would there be enough evidence to convict you?

3. Are you focused? Do ethical standards and an expectation of ethical behavior make the top three strategic initiatives in your global company? Or are they lost somewhere on page 12 of the annual report and page 22 of the employee handbook? No one in the entire General Electric Company has a single doubt that ethics, or Integrity as they refer to it, is one of the very top priorities and expectations of the company, no matter where an employee lives and works worldwide. It is hammered home at every management meeting, at every "Boca" meeting (the annual meeting in January of the top managers and leaders in the company), and it is an issue for which every employee in the company is held accountable. As one GE employee told me during the period of the Joe Jett Kidder Peabody scandal, in 1993, "It feels like a black mark on every single one of us working in this company. It's bad enough that he was responsible for losing so much money for the company, but it's the fact that he single-handedly made us all look like irresponsible employees and, worse, crooks that makes us the maddest."

"There will never be a law against shouting 'Ethics!' in a crowded boardroom. I believe that is so because unlike Fire! yelled in a crowded

theater, the term doesn't possess enough motivational power there to cause a stampede."

... DAVID M. MESSICK

THE STORY OF REEBOK IN ASIA

Scott Thomas is Vice President for Pacific Sourcing and Managing Director, RTFE, for Reebok. Reebok does not "own anything" in Asia, according to Scott, other than computers, desks, and tables:

> We manage our manufacturing requirements through contracts, long-term relationships, and purchasing contracts with factories. The footwear side is quite a bit different than apparel in that we are normally exclusive in these factories. We represent so much business to our company and our needs are fairly unique in that we wouldn't want to develop product alongside of one of our competitors. So we've pretty much got ourselves focused into a one-brand factory; we're exclusive in these manufacturing sources. My responsibility is to manage all those relationships and to assure that we're hitting all our performance marks on quality, delivery, costing, and development of the product. I'm also responsible for positioning ourselves with good solid relationships to carry us forward for the next 5 to 10 years.
>
> If you've been watching any of the recent human rights investigative reporting, we're right in the middle of it, right at the hub of the controversy. Rather than being unfortunate or a huge problem for me, I've actually welcomed it. I've been around this business pretty much since I left college, and I grew up in it. I've watched it move out of Korea and Taiwan and into China, Indonesia, Vietnam, and the Philippines. The amount of focus placed on us by the American media has been tough. I don't think that conditions are nearly as bad as reported, but I think it's well intentioned. It has focused all of us in the business, though particularly in the manufacturing side, as a group of suppliers on areas where we are not as forward, or not as well positioned or as well prepared as we could be. We could have moved ahead quicker on environmental handling, chemical handling, just as we've replaced many hazardous materials with materials less volatile or less hazardous.

It's a kind of weird industry because it hasn't really moved forward technically. I've been around it for almost 20 years, and it's essentially the same process as when I got into it back in 1980. There have been refinements, but there really haven't been any breakthroughs; it's still a very labor-intensive business. There are, in my opinion, way too many hands in it, which has implications for quality control, efficiency, productivity, as well as all the human resource types of issues. It's a little bit frustrating. So that's why it's good to see the attention being put on the industry from outside the sourcing or the buying group to help push things along. It's also an opportunity to make some proactive changes.

Unlike another footwear company I worked with for 10 years, there is a real level of attention and commitment on the area of human rights from the chairman, throughout the senior management group, all the way down to the people we have inspecting the products over here. It's pretty high and pretty deeply felt. There are a lot of people in this company that get upset when they see the entire industry portrayed negatively. As far as management is concerned, there is definitely widespread commitment to improving conditions as rapidly as we can. This other company tends to fight the media. They look at it as a challenge and that they're being misrepresented, the full story isn't being told, the good parts don't get balanced off with the bad.

Scott felt strongly about how the culture of ethical commitment and caring is communicated at Reebok through leadership:

I guess part of it is our corporate heritage. We started with the Reebok Human Rights Award in 1988 in conjunction with Amnesty International. We wanted to structure the awards program to recognize young people throughout the world that resist oppression or are really trying to push forward the envelope in the area of human rights. I think that was the first important element for building communication or building an expression of commitment throughout the company. In 1992 we developed a set of standards for our factories to follow, and that provides a convenient communication vehicle throughout the organization. It says: These are the things we stand for as a company in the area of human rights. These are what our requirements are for any companies that we will do business with as it relates to human rights. You can have a quality-control organization in a company and then all of a sudden *those* guys are responsible for quality.

You've got thousands of people out there around the world who have to be aware of our stand on human rights and how we do business. Although we do have a group in the company that focuses on that, it's actually pretty small, and they primarily help us focus the issues and focus our action planning in the area of human rights. It's really the responsibility of everybody in the organization—our inspectors, production, quality-control people that are in the factory, our development people, all our country managers, everyone—to be responsible for these things.

It's also in everyone's performance objectives and evaluations every year. It's very highly visible, and I think it's well understood by the organization that this is a good thing—the right thing for us to do. Regardless of how we're reported, we're going to continue to push along with programs and plans that we have in place to improve conditions.

THE LESSONS WE'VE LEARNED FROM ORGANIZATIONAL CHANGE EFFORTS

Because we've all been forced to react to, adapt to, or plan for continuous organizational change in the last decade, we've actually looked up long enough to realize that we know some things about successful change at this point. One of the most important lessons we've learned is how important it is to support any identified change with the accompanying systems and structures that support it in a company. In this sense, the term *systems and structures* refers not only to technical systems in a company but also to the entire range of how behaviors are taught, rewarded, compensated, and communicated. How Reebok's human rights priorities are identified for each manager and written into their evaluation plans is an excellent example of how things that are changed are the things that are inspected and expected. The cynic will say that only things that are compensated merit a manager's time, attention, and focus. Another point of view is that creating incentives for certain behaviors helps differentiate true priorities from the morass of activities we are told are important, even when the priorities seem to shift from week to week. Supporting the desired behavior with a company's systems and structures ensures that leadership does not fall into the trap that Steve Kerr, corporate vice president of the General Electric Leadership Development Institute and former professor at the University of Southern California Business School, describes as "the folly of hoping for A while rewarding B"(1975).

According to David M. Messick and Ann E. Tenbrunsel, editors of *Codes of Conduct* (Russell Sage Foundation 1996): Corporations that put in place a corporate code of ethics and do not consider its relationship to existing corporate practices and bonus and promotion systems seem to me to be engaging in window dressing of a particularly cynical sort. Specifically, unless decisions are made that elevate the ethics code over the profit and promotion system, such codes are empty. And in the end, the corporate structure that promulgated the code loses credibility, and its further pronouncements, in the unlikely event they are sincerely intended, will be ignored.

THE IMPORTANCE OF CONSISTENCY OF LEADERSHIP

Mary Ann Pearce, vice president at Conoco International Natural Gas reflected:

> We do business in some typically corrupt places, but I've never been offered a bribe, at least that I've noticed. I think there are a couple of reasons for that. First, the Foreign Corrupt Practices Act has been around for a while now, and it's getting better known in the countries and with the suppliers and customers we do business with. But more importantly, DuPont's reputation is known here. People are sizing you up all the time, they watch you. They watch your body language and how you interact with people here in every possible situation. If I'd come on board and been a "rounder" and given off different signals about what I'd be open to, then I think the story might be different. We spend a lot of time with our legal people, because we want to make sure that the language we use in any of our communications and documents doesn't inadvertently mislead people here.

Michael Morgan, of Conoco, agrees:

Ultimately the main enforcer of ethical behavior is the culture of this company. It's visible everywhere in our leadership. People in other countries know that in the procurement group DuPont accepts nothing—ever! They all know that. It took a while to develop that reputation, and it meant that we had to be absolutely consistent across the board at every instance. It makes our dealings much easier today.

Scott Thomas, of Reebok says:

You know, we've been at this in Asia for a while now. These relationships we have with the factories are fairly long term and they have a lot at stake, too, by this point. In every region we have to demonstrate our level of integrity. I send out a couple of reminders a couple times of year to all the factories. We'll reiterate our factory standards and codes of compliance and our gift policy, what we find acceptable and what we don't find acceptable. I ask all our suppliers to respond back by letter that they understand and that they will comply with the policy. We started this back in 1995 or 1996, but I guess the concept goes back to the early 1980s. You get some factories that don't work well with you. They'll sign the letter, and at Lunar New Year you'll find this wine and cheese in your office. The guys just don't get it. I was talking with some friends from other companies who buy a lot of product here as well—from factories in the Far East who really have problems. We don't really have a problem because we send such a strong message that it's not acceptable. That's what we've had to do over the years, keep reinforcing that. The more you send back the better that message drives home.

Joe Wertheim has been in the tea business for 50 years. While living in New York during the Depression, Joe took a job washing tea cups in the tea tasting room of a large importer in the city. Today he is president of the privately held company Tea Importers, Inc., founded in 1953 and headquartered in Westport, Connecticut. Tea Importers, Inc. imports tea from all the major and many of the minor tea-producing countries in the world, buying tea in 20 countries and selling it worldwide to blenders. Mr. Wertheim has had to do business in many of the countries that come up on the bottom end of the corruption index, including India, Africa, Sri Lanka, and Indonesia. His company is the only U.S. tea company with investments in tea-producing countries, including a tea estate in Rwanda which produces 6 million pounds of high-quality tea. Because Wertheim runs a processing plant with 200 to 250 employees and has 1,000 employees in the field, I was curious about how he and his company, consisting of managers, agents, and field workers, has managed to steer clear of the all-too-present and publicized business corruption in Africa. Said Joe:

> We told them early. No graft. No corruption. It certainly took us longer to negotiate our original contract that way—3 years altogether. And since then we have simply refused every time we were approached or asked to participate or collude. Now they don't ask. We're a known quantity today. Initially they all had their hands out. We don't pay off anybody, and they know that today.

This idea of being a known quantity for ethical behavior was a concept and a phrase that came up repeatedly among all sorts of companies when they described how they managed consistently to conduct business ethically in some of the most admittedly corrupt countries in the world. Devon Archer, the young Direct Investment Manager at Citibank Vietnam commented on this aspect of the importance of strong leadership in this difficult and complicated area:

> Our ethics code is like every other ethics code for every company I've ever seen or worked for. The people more than the structure of the document are what's important in the code. It's how they adopt the code and their sense of ethics. Ethics is more the feeling that Citibank is going to provide well for all of us. Let's not do anything to jeopardize this or jeopardize the business when things are working well. Let's just keep behaving the way we've been behaving that's gotten us this far and so well.
>
> Recently a new corporate identity and branding process was launched with Citibank. This sense of who we are is a collective feeling. It definitely comes from the leadership, this ethical direction we have. And it's the older guys, surprisingly, who seem to care the most. You see the senior leadership staying within the boundaries. I'll ask my boss, "Can I do that?" and

they'll say no, but they're not suspicious or punitive, just helpful. They'll tell stories like about that guy from Barings Bank and say how it is wrong and why. That's how our leadership works around here.

Regardless of the policies in place or the training videos that have been shown, most managers want to turn or be able to turn to their immediate managers for advice and counsel in matters about ethical dilemmas. This is another reason why good communication and a variety of personal vehicles have to be established. Managers and employees need to feel that they can talk openly about their questions, anxieties, and things that disturb them. Employees need to feel that their managers will not consider their questions indications of lack of knowledge or confidence. Two such examples come from Peg Urda, director of global training and organization development for American Cyanamid, a chemical company of American Home Products, and our friend at Reebok, Scott Thomas.

As part of her assignment, Peg Urda designs and develops new programs specifically for Cyanamid's international business marketing programs. "So much is changing in our business, just like almost every other business," comments Peg when she describes the issues facing her company and the chemical industry. "We face increasing competition. For a long time we've had a technology advantage, now there are more competitors coming into the market. In addition, prices are decreasing and the markets themselves are changing. We shifted how we do business with customers and agents at the same time that our distributor's network is increasing and getting stronger outside the U.S. It's an increasing challenge to grow our business and our profit earnings." Peg and other managers were prepared for traveling and business in other countries through attending a course about conducting business internationally. Even so, she has been surprised at times to encounter some of the issues of doing business in other cultures. "Recently I was met in Columbia with two separate cars. This was done for security reasons, I was told. The second car was a 'back up' in case we needed it." Even though Peg's trips and business dealings have gone smoothly for the most part, she knows she could encounter some difficult situations that her Human Resource colleagues in a particular country may not be able to handle. "Whenever I have an issue that I need guidance on or which causes some anxiety for me, I go straight to the Vice President for Global Business." This inclination and desire to seek counsel and assistance from one's manager is a reminder of how important that relationship is for global managers. We can only hope that these managers to whom we are all turning have a grounded sense of how to assess and resolve the situation and provide support.

Recalls Scott Thomas, of Reebok:

When I first got to Korea, I was 23 years old and working for another footwear company. I was heading off on my first vacation, and the fellow that I interact with most directly at the factory, an English speaker and someone I could communicate [with] about basic business issues, but Korean, comes up with an envelope with a bunch of money in it—$1,000.00! "What's this?" I asked him and he said, "It's for your vacation." It was almost comical. I was completely taken aback. The Korean colleague told me that whenever one of our people goes on vacation they give him some extra money to spend. I told him this just wasn't something I did. But I was 22, 23 years old and really stunned! I went to the fellow who was the general manager of the office and asked him what I should do about this. He asked me what I did with the money, and I told him it was still sitting in my desk and I didn't want to touch it.

The general manager asked Scott why he didn't give the money back. I told him the guy wouldn't go until he could leave it. He sneaked it under my files so he could go. You know, in a later conversation with the Korean colleague he told me he would have lost face with his boss if he hadn't left it. "My boss made me come and give that to you so we can build our relationship," he stated emphatically. Now the general manager told me that this was a traditional thing in Korea and that they'd had to deal with it before. "What we normally do," the manager told me, "is we take the money and put it into an office kitty during Christmas time or one of the other holidays, and we'll use that to fund an office party. " I still felt funny about that—I didn't think it was okay. Consequently, the man that was the general manager was found to have taken more than just the vacation money and he was let go from the company. I don't know exactly what the investigations turned up. Anyway, I guess he wasn't the best person to go to as a mentor!

These early experiences influenced how Scott behaves as a manager today:

Today I just do the uncomfortable thing and I give the money back. Sometimes it's right at the point when it is offered, sometimes it's putting it in an envelope when I get back to the office and sending it back with my driver or somebody else—I always completely refuse it. It isn't necessarily a problem for me since I have been in positions of running a country, but I do think about the 23-year-olds we have coming over here today and working in this environment. I think it's a real important communication to get across to everyone in the organization that this just isn't—regardless of what the cultural connotations are—it really isn't acceptable for us as employees of an American company, or as human beings, to put ourselves in a position where we're compromising our ethics because of a particular situation, because we felt it was good for a particular business relationship or because we feel that culturally we've got to do it to be accepted. The time this is most difficult is when you have a personal relationship with someone in your office and you know it will put them in a bad light with their boss. I frequently got the argument, "President Park is a very traditional Korean, and he absolutely would not accept that you'd turn this down." That's hard.

LEADERSHIP BEHAVIORS THAT BUILD ETHICAL COMPETENCE

What have these managers and others told us about Best Practices in leadership behaviors that build ethical competence? What follows are practices compiled from the stories and experiences of managers in global companies. Later in this chapter I discuss the importance of building communities of ethical leadership and why that is the most important role leaders can play in developing ethical competence in their organizations.

A leader always has choices. It is the pattern of those choices that play a large part in determining the style or reputation a

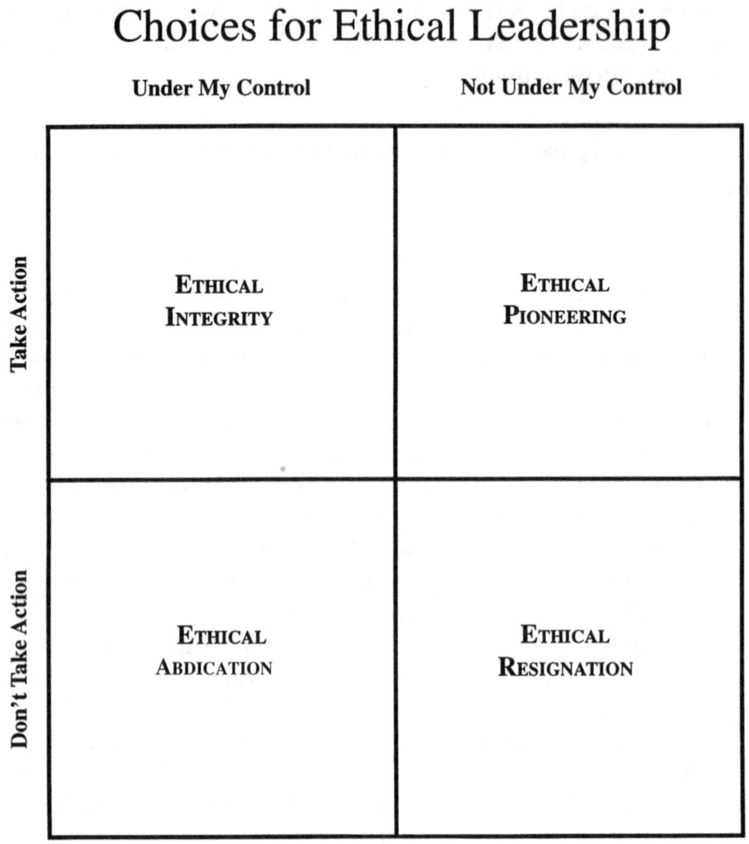

Choices for Ethical Leadership

	Under My Control	Not Under My Control
Take Action	ETHICAL INTEGRITY	ETHICAL PIONEERING
Don't Take Action	ETHICAL ABDICATION	ETHICAL RESIGNATION

Figure 6.2 Choices for Ethical Leadership

leader develops in navigating difficult issues of any kind in an organization. The diagram above illustrates the basic choices and outcomes for ethical decision making on the part of leaders.

Ethical Integrity

I am doing everything possible under my control to build ethical competence in my organization and deal effectively and directly with the issues presented from individuals and organizations from other cultures. This is the area of ethical competence where corporate policies and organizational practices such as mentoring processes and systems, cross-cultural dialogues, live cases, and reward and compensation practices are identified and implemented. This is also the arena where straightforward yesses and nos are heard, emphasized, and reemphasized. This is where developing your self and your organization as a known quantity comes into play. Writer and speaker Parker J. Palmer describes why the act of acting is so powerful: "Through action we both express and learn something of who we are, of the kind of world we have or want. Action…is the visible form of an invisible spirit, an outward manifestation of an inward power. But as we act, we not only express what is in us and help give shape to the world; we also receive what is outside us, and we reshape our inner selves. When we act, the world acts back, and we and the world are cocreated"(Palmer 1990). When we step into our power by taking action when it is required and when it is most available to us, we become the manifestation of ethical competence to both ourselves and those with whom we must engage. When we do this consistently, both we as individuals and the organizations we represent start to build the foundations for becoming a known quantity, and the cornerstones of integrity and credibility are laid.

Ethical Abdication

The problem is under my control or influence but I don't take any action. This arena of ethical abdication is where many of the dilemmas lie that turn into public issues, scandals, and interpersonal tension and conflict. If I know the right thing to do and I don't do that right thing, then I have abdicated my role as a leader, a mentor, and an ethical human being. If I do not take deliberate action in a timely manner, the message communicated to my organization is that ethical quibbling is acceptable. The personal wear and tear of this constant struggle is usually borne by the individual manager trying to operate under this lack of leadership.

Ethical Pioneering

The problem is not under my control, but I want to try to influence it positively. As a leader I may try to meet one on one with specific individuals and attempt to reach new agreements. A consortium of leading global companies that have been meeting for several years to mitigate widespread corruption in countries recently announced a new agreement and made a public statement about where the acceptable norms will be. General Electric attempted to tackle this issue of systemic corruption by taking out full-page advertisement in local papers in Indonesia to condemn it. Ethical pioneers also make sure they have done everything possible to put effective internal systems and structures in place within the organization to be able to meet and deal with ethical issues and dilemmas of individuals in the organization. (Continuous, fruitless "pioneering" however, also can be perceived as public moralizing and can lead to ethical wheel-spinning.)

Ethical Resignation

The ethical problems are overwhelming and completely out of my control, and I couldn't do anything about it anyway even if I wanted to. This quadrant is fertile ground for cynics and individuals, or organizations that just "go along with it" because they truly believe there is no choice.

THE ESSENTIAL ROLE OF TRUST IN NAVIGATING CROSS-CULTURAL ETHICS

As I work with companies and managers around the world and talk to many more about these complex issues of ethics in global companies, I am repeatedly struck by the simplicity, rather than the complexity, of the issues involved. Inevitably, the main issues worth caring about are issues of trust.

Trust Yourself

You need to trust that you can acquire the information you need to not embarrass yourself or your company. It's up to you to determine the best sources of information but what managers have told us is that there is good, concrete information to be gained from reading books on cross-cultural business, viewing training films, talking with people who have already worked in that culture, and watching your own inner gyroscope to see what feels right and what does not. Advice from those in the trenches is never to ignore inner signals that go off as ethical warning systems. When the system goes off, seek help and advice, talk to your manager—whatever it takes. But listen to the warning bells and do not assume you should go through the dilemma and struggle alone. To navigate cross-culture ethics successfully, you have to be able to trust yourself.

Trust Your Organization

You have to be able to trust your leadership and the leadership of your organization. You need to know that you can talk about the issues you confront, and that you will not be punished or penalized for looking for answers when the company may feel you should already know them. Clear and meaningful policies and practices, clear channels of communication for dealing with ethical dilemmas and violations, and clear examples of consistent leadership in action all contribute to a sense of trust in one's organization.

Trust Your Global Partners

One aspect of navigating cross-cultural ethics that we have not looked at in depth is relationships with specific business partners. Companies that have dealt with partners over a period of years as suppliers, manufacturers, and customers have reported the long-term advantages of relationship building on both ends of the transaction. One component of ethical pioneering is making an assumption of trust and operating on that assumption until the evidence indicates that more caution is required. Caution is not intended to substitute for sound practices, but it is the flip side and more positive alternative to suspicion as a way of being.

Norbert Roobaert is president of Alliance Engineering, a company based in Houston, Texas, that does engineering work all over the world. Norb considers the element of trust in global partners absolutely germane to effective and ethical business practices. Norb described several large transactions he has been involved with in Russia and China:

> From a practical standpoint, if they don't trust you or you don't trust them, or you don't do the job that they thought you were going to do, or they don't pay you, and you think they should pay you, then basically there's not much you're going to do anyway. If they don't think that we're going a good job and they shouldn't pay us then they don't pay us and we stop working. There's not a whole lot the lawyers can do about it.
>
> A lot of this is done as a matter of trust. When you get lawyers involved they look for things that can go wrong if your partner doesn't do what they say they're going to do. Then what are you going to do? So much of this is a matter of trust. I do business with them, and we need to trust each other to work out an agreement. It may take longer than we think it should, or it may be done in a process that looks different from what we'd do, but we have to trust that it will eventually emerge.

Ultimately what we are striving for through using all the tools for building ethical competence is creation in our global business interactions of a community of ethical practice. The term *communities of practice* was first coined by Etienne Wenger and Jean Lave in their 1991 book *Situated Learning*. Wenger writes in his forthcoming book *Communities of Practice: Learning, Meaning, and Identity* (1998) that

> communities of practice include both the explicit and the tacit. It includes what is said and what is left unsaid; what is represented and what is assumed. It includes the language, the tools, the documents, the images, the symbols, the well-defined roles, the codified procedures, the regulations, and the contracts that various practices make explicit for a variety of purposes. But it also includes all the implicit relations, the tacit conventions, the subtle cues, the untold rules of thumb, the recognizable intuitions, the specific perceptions, the well-tuned sensitivities, the embodied understandings, the underlying assumptions, the shared worldviews, which may never be articulated, though they are unmistakable signs of membership in communities of practice and are crucial to the success of their enterprises.

To have a community of ethical practice means to be aware of all these factors—tacit and spoken, content- and technically oriented (such as laws, codes, regulations), and intuitive and process oriented (relationships, trust) and to make all that knowledge available to the other members of the community. A community of ethical practice expands the ethical practices of isolated individuals until those practices become a critical mass of shared behavior and common vision.

The playing field of business and ethics in global companies is changing and already looks quite different from the way it did 20 years ago. The Foreign Corrupt Practices Act is more well known in countries in which corruption traditionally has been a pervasive business problem. As emerging global economies become players in the new economic order, they have substantially more to lose by continuing the corrupt practices that alienate western companies. An increasing number of large companies now have track records of 20 years or more in many of the traditionally corrupt countries. The consistent ethical behavior of walking away from the table or simply refusing to engage in corrupt practices has allowed a new community of ethical practice to emerge in these regions. An increasing number of companies are learning how to develop *global brains* (a term derived from the General Electric values) and are increasingly moving from tactics of Survival to tactics of Understanding and Knowing in their interactions with their global business partners.

FINAL THOUGHTS

When we live in a world of whitewater, we simply cannot predict every interaction, every situation, or every problem in every country. Even if it were humanly possible to freeze-frame the world and all the components that interact with each other and affect each other, the data would be good for no longer than a millisecond. As soon as we were to push the Play button and began again, many of the elements would be changed, obsolete, nonexistent.

Devon Archer, of Citibank Vietnam, reflected about his experiences of being immersed in the business ethics of Vietnam:

> Each month I look back on the previous month and say, God, I didn't know anything! And in fact, you can never be prepared, even if you thought you knew everything everyday. There's a curve ball thrown not once a day, but ten times a day. If you try to know everything and read everything about a country, you're doomed. I read everywhere all the time, but it's still the day-to-day that's the best teacher. You've got to be overprepared to be underprepared.

If it is true that we can never be fully prepared to deal with the dilemmas and "curves" of navigating ethical differences in global companies, and I believe that is true, what is our challenge as leaders in these companies? For what are we truly accountable?

I believe we must intentionally set the conditions in organizations that support ethical choices; conditions that support our cultural, political, religious, and corporate values in the United States; conditions that allow us to give in to our higher instincts, our intuitive knowledge about ourselves, and what is right for us and for our organizations. We can begin to build communities of practice brick by brick with each act of mentoring a younger or newer person, each invitation for dialogue about differences—in our own companies or across companies and cultures—and with each invitation to another to take ethical action.

"Ethics is how we behave when [we believe that] we belong together."
. . . FATHER DAVID STENDL-RAST
BRACKETS INDICATE EDITING BY MARGARET WHEATLEY
AND MYRON KELLNER-ROGERS

"We are all in this thing together—individually."
. . . LILY TOMLIN

References

Abratt, R., Nel, D. and Higgs, N. S. (1992). "An Examination of the Ethical Beliefs of Managers Using Selected Scenarios in a Cross-Cultural Environment." *Journal of Business Ethics*, 11(1), 29–35.

Ashkenas, R., Ulrich, D., Jick, T. and Kerr, S. (1995). *The Boundaryless Organization: Breaking the Chains of Organizational Structure.* San Francisco, CA: Jossey-Bass.

Badaracco, J. L., Jr. (1997). *Defining Moments: When Managers Must Choose between Right and Right.* Cambridge, MA: Harvard Business School Press.

Barry, V. (1985). *Applying Ethics: A Text with Readings,* Second edition. San Francisco, CA: Wadsworth.

Burrows, P, Bernier, L, Engardio, P. "Chipmakers: Texas Instruments' Global Chip Payoff." *Business Week,* August 7, 1995.

Carr, A. Z. "Is Business Bluffing Ethical?" *Harvard Business Review,* January/February 1968.

Chekov, A. (1968). *The Major Plays.* New York: Signet.

Churchill, L. R. (1982). "The Teaching of Ethics and Moral Values in Teaching: Some Contemporary Confusions." *Journal of Higher Education,* 53 (3), 296–306.

"Company Watch." *Business Ethics Magazine.* March-April 1998, p. 7.

Donaldson, T. (1989). *The Ethics of International Business.* New York: Oxford Press.

Donaldson, T. "Values in Tension." *Harvard Business Review,* September-October, 1996, pp. 48–62.

Donaldson, T. (1998). *Business Ethics as Social Contracts.* Boston: Harvard Business School Press.

Dwyer, P., Engardio, P., Schiller, Z., Reed, S. "Tomorrow's Winners Will Use Western-style Accounting, Japanese-style Teamwork, Advanced Communications–and Give Entrepreneurial Local Managers a Long Leash," *Business Week,* November 18, 1994.

Fowler, J. W. (1981). *Stages of Faith.* San Francisco, CA: Harper & Row.

Goodall, K. (1994). "1994 Ethics in American Business Survey." The Ethics Resource Center, Washington, DC.

Green, R. M. (1994). *The Ethical Manager: A New Method for Business Ethics.* New York: Macmillan College Publishing Co.

Harte, B. (1896). *The Crusade of the Excelsior: And Other Tales.* Boston: Houghton-Mifflin.

Hillman, James (1989). *Blue Fire.* New York: Harper Perennial.

Hofstede, G. (1984). *Culture's Consequences.* Newbury Park, CA: Sage Publishing.

"International Fraud Report." KPMG International Forensic Accounting Network. April 1996.

Kazakov, A. (1992). Unpublished research paper in progress.

Kegan, R. (1994). *In Over Our Heads: The Mental Demands of Modern Life.* Cambridge, MA: Harvard University Press.

Kegan, R. (1982). *The Evolving Self.* Cambridge: Harvard University Press.

Kerr, S. "On the Folly of Rewarding A, while Hoping for B." *Academy of Management Journal,* 1975, pp 769–783.

Kidder, R. M. (1994). *Shared Values for a Troubled World.* San Francisco, CA: Jossey-Bass.

Kohlberg, L. (1984). *The Psychology of Moral Development.* New York: Harper & Row.

Light, L. "Downsizers Still Wield a Mean Ax," *Business Week,* May 20, 1996.

Messick, D. M. and Tenbrunsel, A. E. (1996). *Codes of Conduct: Behavioral Research into Business Ethics.* New York: Russell Sage Foundation.

Miller, A. (1957). *Arthur Miller's Collected Plays.* New York: Viking.

Moody, H. R. (1997). *The Five Stages of the Soul.* New York: Anchor Books/Doubleday.

Morgan, E. (1995). *An Exploration of the Meaning of Business Ethics in a Cross-Cultural Context with Russians and Americans.* Ann Arbor, MI: UMI.

Nash, L. L. (1993). *Good Intentions Aside: A Manager's Guide to Resolving Ethical Problems.* Cambridge, MA: Harvard Business School Press.

Palmer, P. (1991) *The Active Life.* San Francisco, CA: Harper.

Richards, L. (1998). *The Heart of Knowledge: An Epistemology of Relationship.* Ann Arbor, MI: UMI.

Rolle, A. F. (1929). *California: A History.* New York: Crowell.

Said, E. W. (1993). *Culture and Imperialism.* New York: Alfred A. Knopf.

Slater, R. (1994). *Get Better or Get Beaten.* New York: Irwin Professional Publishing.

Stacey, R. D. (1992). *Managing the Unknowable: Strategic Boundaries between Order and Chaos in Organizations.* San Francisco, CA: Jossey-Bass.

Talbot, M. (1991). *The Holographic Universe.* New York: Harper Collins.

Thurow, L. (1996). *Keynote Speech: International Strategic Management Conference.* May 1996, Atlanta, GA.

Thurow, L. (1996). *The Future of Capitalism: How Today's Economic Forces Shape Tomorrow's World.* New York: William Morrow & Co.

Tichy, N. and Sherman, S. (1993). *Control Your Destiny or Someone Else Will.* New York: Currency Doubleday.

Tourevski, M. and Morgan, E. (1993) *Cutting the Red Tape: How Western Companies Can Profit in the New Russia.* New York: The Free Press.

Treece, J. B., Kerwin, K., Dawley, H. "Ford: Alex Trotman's Daring Global Strategy," *Business Week,* April 3, 1995.

U.S. Department of Commerce, Bureau of Economic Analysis (April 9, 1998 update)
(1) "U.S. International Trade in Goods and Services Balance of Payments (BOP)"
(2) "U.S. total Exports to Individual Countries, 1991–1997"
(3) "U.S. Total Imports From Individual Countries, 1991–1997"

Vaill, Peter. (1989). *Managing as a Performing Art.* San Francisco, CA: Jossey Bass.

Wegner, E. and Lave, J. (1991). *Situated Learning.* Cambridge, UK: Cambridge University Press.

Wegner, E. (1998). *Communities of Practice: Learning, Meaning, and Identity.* Cambridge, UK: Cambridge University Press.

Wheatley, M. (1992). *Leadership and the New Science.* San Francisco, CA: Berrett-Kohler.

Wines, W. A. and Napier, N. K. (1992). "Toward an Understanding of Cross-Cultural Ethics: A Tentative Model. *Journal of Business Ethics,* 11, pp. 831–841.

World Business Perspective, (Sept/Oct 1996), p.31.

Appendix I

*Business Ethics
Organizations and Institutes*

Center for Business Ethics
  http://www.bentley.edu/resource/cbe/

The Center for Business Ethics is dedicated to promoting ethical business conduct in contempoary society. With a vast network of practitioners and scholars, and an expansive multimedia library, the center provides an international forum for benchmarking and research in business ethics. The center helps corporations and other organizations strengthen their ethical cultures through educational programming and consulting.

Center for Business Ethics
Adamian Graduate Center,
Room 108
Bentley College
Waltham, Massachusetts, 0245:
Telephone: 781/891-2981
FAX: 781/891-2988
E-mail: cbeinfo@bentley.edu

Who Are We?

- History and Mission
- Programs and Projects
- Funding
- Staff (Pincus Hartman/Koehn home pages)
- Membership
- Sponsoring Partners
- Corporate members
- Information about Chicago

Media/press representatives, please click here for more information.

History and Mission

The Institute for Business & Professional Ethics was established in 1985 by a joint effort of the Colleges of Liberal Arts and Sciences and Commerce at DePaul University. The Institute is one of the first ethics-related resources to pioneer a hypertext linked ethics network throughout the Internet.

- The mission of the IBPE is to encourage ethical deliberation in decision-makers by stirring the moral conscience and imagination.
- Our objective is to provide a forum for exploring and furthering ethical practices in organizations.
- Our goals are therefore to provide ethics-related programming and to offer quality resources such as a website, conferences, lecture series, on-site training, discussion, and written and electronic publications.

The Institute recognizes that it, too, is an ethical actor. Therefore, the Institute strives to make exemplary responsible contributions to the lives of the civic, social and economic stakeholders it serves. The Institute contributes by:

- 1. Annually reviewing its programs and curricula to ensure congruence with its Mission.
- 2. Annually challenging its stakeholders to scrutinize their practices.
- 3. Providing for and participating in ethics-related education and offering resources to our stakeholders (e.g. conferences, lecture series, on-site training, discussion and written materials).
- 4. Developing teachers skilled in the formation of ethical agents.
- 5. Supporting and disseminating cutting-edge scholarship of ethical relevance.
- 6. Locating resources to support the above objectives.

Our Programs and Projects

The Institute is a partner with the Philosophy Department's Center for Human Values, which serves as a focal point of its Ph.D. program. In addition, the Institute supports, facilitates or coordinates a number of programs each year which seek to serve the goal of our Mission. The programs supported by the Institute are not intended to reflect one common approach to ethics pedagogy or training, but instead exemplify the Institute's commitment to the teaching of business ethics from a variety of perspectives. We hope that this approach will stimulate one's moral imagination to view possibilities never before considered.

For example, during the academic year, 1994-1995, the Institute helped to coordinate a series of three workshops in DePaul's College of Commerce seeking to encourage Commerce faculty to integrate ethics teaching and discussion in their courses. Also, along with St. John's and Niagara Universities, the Institute sponsors an annual conference on teaching and training in business ethics for academic scholars and practitioners.

Funding

The Institute is funded through several sources, including DePaul University's Colleges of Commerce and Liberal Arts & Sciences, membership fees, and individual or corporate donations. As the Institute has no permanent endowment, we welcome offers of additional support and are willing to discuss the possibility of grants to support its programming for the benefit of students, faculty and the corporate community.

Staff

The Institute's Director is Laura Pincus Hartman, an associate professor of legal studies and ethics in DePaul's College of Commerce and the Wicklander Chair in Professional Ethics. Hartman has published extensively on the topic of ethics in the employment relationship and has won the university's Excellence in Teaching Award.

The Institute's Administrator is Thekla Tsonis.

Members of the Board of Directors include business professionals from firms such as Sears, Amoco, AT&T and Walgreens.

Membership

To become a member of the Institute for Business & Professional Ethics, click here.

Ethics Home
Site Directory | What's New?
About the Institute | Ethics Calendar
Ethics Resources | Professional Resources | Ethics Beat | DePaul Home
Copyright© 1997 Institute for Business and Professional Ethics. All rights reserved.

Comments and questions: On Ethics, lpincus@wppost.depaul.edu, or on the creation of this site, dthies@wppost.depaul.edu

About EBEN [European Business Ethics Network]

Contents

Introduction

the framework of our world is changing...

Political, economic and social structures considered immutable only a few years ago have altered out of all recognition. Concern for the environment has moved from being the preserve of a few small radical groups to being a mainstream business issue.

Within organisations -both public and private sector- these changes are often paralleled by flatter management structures and new ways of working -a focus on quality and customer service delivered by teams of empowered employees.

Managing organisational relationships and issues in this constantly mutating process is complex and difficult.

Ensuring that decisions are right not only in profit terms but also in ethical terms may require a new approach.

The discipline of business ethics, firmly established for two decades in the United States as well as in Europe, can offer support to companies who wish to manage these issues actively.
Business ethics can provide:

- a framework for decision making in specific situations
- tools and insights to tackle questions transcending individual companies
- for organisations taking a long term-view, new ideas regarding the role of business and of the public sector in shaping future society

Founded in 1987, **EBEN** is a not-for-profit association. Our network members include business people, public sector managers, and academics. Our role is to stimulate and facilitate meetings of minds, discussion and debate on common ethical problems and dilemmas. We do this in the following ways:

- Annual Conference
  Publications
- Research Centres Meeting
- National Networks

ASSOCIATION FOR
Practical and Professional Ethics

618 East Third Street, Bloomington, Indiana 47405
(812) 855-6450 | FAX (812) 855-3315 | appe@indiana.edu
Brian Schrag, Executive Secretary

- Aims of the Association Benefits of membership, applying for membership, . . .
- Activities Annual meeting, workshops, . . .
- Publications Newsletter, *Profiles in Ethics*, cases on research ethics, . . .
- Electronic Networking E-mail distribution lists, other links, . . .

Association Activities

- Ethics in the Professions and Practice, August 2-6, 1998
- Eighth Annual Meeting, February 25-27, 1999, *Meeting Announcement and Call for Papers*
- Regional Meeting, Chico, California, October 16-17, 1998
- Graduate Research Ethics Education, June 3-7, 1998

Association Publications

- *Research Ethics: Cases and Commentaries*
- *Ethically Speaking* -- a semiannual newsletter
- *Profiles in Ethics* -- a comprehensive list of member ethics centers
- Directory of members
- Oxford University Press Series in Practical and Professional Ethics (sponsored by the Association)

Electronic Networking Opportunities

- APPE_ETHICSNET -- E-mail bulletins from the Association (notices of job openings, seminars, calls for papers, fellowships, etc.)
- APPE_PRACNET -- Members of the Association may join this discussion list. Ask pedagogical questions, share techniques, discuss issues with other Association members.
- Send an e-mail message to the Association for more information.
- Links to other World Wide Web sites.

Association for Practical and Professional Ethics
618 East Third Street
Bloomington, Indiana 47405
(812) 855-6450
FAX (812) 855-3315
APPE@INDIANA.EDU

Other Institutes

http://www.depaul.edu/ethics/ethi1.html ————————————————

The Academy of Legal Studies in Business
   http://miavx1.muohio.edu/~herrondj
The Academy of Management Online
   http://www.aom.pace.edu/
American Philosophy Association Home Page
   http://www.oxy.edu/apa/apa.html
The Association for Practical and Professional Ethics
   http://ezinfo.ucs.indiana.edu/~appe/home.html
The Beard Center for Leadership in Ethics
The Bioethics Centre at University of Alberta
   http://www.ualberta.ca/ethics/bethics.htm
BIONEERS
   http://www.bioneers.org/
Business Enterprise Trust
   http://www.betrust.org/
Center for The Advancement of Ethics
   http://www.uwyo.edu/bu/acct/cae.htm
Center for the Advancement of Applied Ethics
   http://www.lcl.cmu.edu/CAAE/Home/CAAE.html
The Center for Business Ethics at Bentley College
   http://www.bentley.edu/resource/cbe
Center for Ethics, University of Tampa
   Mailto: Debbie Thorne
Center for Ethics in the Sciences and Humanities (University of Tuebingen)
   http://www.uni-tuebingen.de/zew/index_e.htm
Center for Medical Ethics and Mediation
   www.wh.com/cmem
Center for Applied & Professional Ethics, Central Missouri State University
   http://www.cmsu.edu/englphil/center.html
The Center for Professional and Applied Ethics
   University of North Carolina at Charlotte
   Phone: (704) 547-3542 Fax: (704) 547-2172
The Center of Professional Ethics at Manhattan College
   http://www.manhattan.edu/special/prethics/corporat.html
The Centre for Research Ethics
   http://www.cre.gu.se/homepage/
Center for the Study of Great Ideas
   http://www.npcts.edu/~mj_adler
The Centre for Sustainable Design
   http://www.cfsd.org.uk/
The Chinmaya Institute of Management (CIM)
   http://www.chinmaya.org/centers/india/CIM.html
The Computer Ethics Institute

http://www.brook.edu/sscc/cei/cei_hp.htm
Computer Professionals for Social Responsibility
   http://cpsr.org/home/
Consortium Ethics Program, Univ. of Pittsburgh Center for Medical Ethics
   http://www.pitt.edu/~caj3/CEP.html
Council on Economic Priorities
   http://www.envirolink.org/pbn/cep
Electronic Frontier Foundation
   http://www.eff.org/
Ethics Resouce Center
   http://www.ethics.org/
֍ Ethics Updates
   http://ethics.acusd.edu/
➤European Business Ethics Network (EBEN)
   http://www.nijenrode.nl/research/eibe/eben/
Gaia's Hive: The Ethics Reource Center
   http://www.per2per.com/
Harvard University, Program for Ethics and The Professions
   http://condor.depaul.edu/ethics/harvard.html
The Heartland Institute
   http://www.heartland.org
Hoffberger Center for Professional Ethics
   Dr. Fred Guy, Director
   University of Baltimore
   1420 North Charles Street, AC#204
   Baltimore, MD 21201
   410-837-5324
IIT's Center for Ethics in the Professions
   http://www.iit.edu/~csep
Institute for Business Ethics of the University of St. Gallen
   http://www.unisg.ch/~iwe/english/homepage.htm
Institute for Global Communication
   http://www.igc.apc.org/
Institute for Global Ethics, Camden, MN
   http://www.globalethics.org
The Institute of Practical Philosophy
   http://www.mala.bc.ca/www/ipp/ipp.htm
Inst. for Study of Applied and Professional Ethics at Dartmouth College
   http://www.dartmouth.edu/artsci/ethics-inst/
International Association for Business and Society and the Social Issues in Management Division of
the Academy of Management.
   http://cac.psu.edu/~plc/iabs.html
The Josephson Institute (Information on "Ethics Corps")
   http://www.josephsoninstitute.org.
The Josephson's youth-ethics initiative
   http://www.charactercounts.org
The Marketing Resource Center
   http://www.marketingsource.com/

The Markkula Center for Applied Ethics (an enormous database of "Ethical Links" on the web)
http://www.scu.edu/Ethics/
Murray G. Bacon Center for Ethics in Business, Iowa State University
http://www.public.iastate.edu/~BACON_CENTER?homepage.html
National Institute of Ethics
Mailto: Ethics@acc.net
The Olsson Center for Applied Ethics, Darden School, University of Virginia
http:// www.darden.virginia.edu/research/olsson/olsson.htm
Ontario Centre for Religious Tolerance
http://www.kosone.com/people/ocrt/ocrt_hp.htm
Pacific Research Institute
http://www.ideas.org
Philosophy Departments On-Line
University of Indiana
California Lutheran University Philosophy Department
Poynter Center for the Study of Ethics in American Institutions
http://gopher.indiana.edu:2002/poynter/gopher
The Ridley Hall Foundation
http://users.aol.com/faithwork/ridley-1.htm
Religious Research Centre
http://www.jetlink.com.ph/users/religion/rrc.html
The Society for Business Ethics and Business Ethics Quarterly
http://www.luc.edu/depts/business/sbe/index.htm
The Southwetern Legal Foudation (Includes The Southwestern Law Enforcement Institute and
Center for Law Enforcement Ethics)
http://web2.airmail.net/slf/
St. Antoninus Institute for Catholic Education in Business
http://www.ewtn.org/antonin/antonin.htm
The St. James Ethics Center
Email: Simon Longstaff
Thunderbird Institute for International Business Ethics
http://www2.mgmt.purdue.edu/Centers/CIBER/schools/thndrbrd/tbethics.htm
Transparency International (coalition against corruption in international business)
http://www.transparency.de/
The UBC Centre for Applied Ethics
http://www.ethics.ubc.ca/
University of Leeds Centre for Business and Professional Ethics
U.N.L.V. Institute for Ethics and Policy Studies
Mailto: Sparks@nevada.edu
WDHB, Inc. organizes Learning Expeditions for Executive Teams, on topics such as: The Spirit of
Service, Exemplarity and Ethics at the Top.
http://www.wdhb.com/
The Wharton Ethics Program
http://rider.wharton.upenn.edu/~ethics/
The Wheaton College Center for Apllied Ethics
http://www.wheaton.edu/CACE
The Woodstock Theological Center
http://guweb.georgetown.edu/woodstock/

WWW Ethics Center for Engineering & Science

http://web.mit.edu/ethics/www/
E-Mail: Caroline Whitbeck

Appendix II

Ethics Management Consultants

Ethics/Management Consultants

Character Training Institute (CTI)

Character education courses
Courses are taught in a seminar format which allows proactive, guided interaction between group members and the facilitator. Active participation by everyone is encouraged. The setting is informal, relaxed, and fun. The content is relative to the participant's situations and will address the special ethical dilemmas confronting employees in their workplace. The teaching format includes active discussion, inspirational readings and stories, hypothetical situations, media presentations, role play, and lots of fun!

COUNCIL FOR ETHICS IN ECONOMICS

Sixteen years of helping leaders of varied institutions (corporations, governments, hospitals, etc.) successfully address ethical issues in the workplace is the foundation of the Council's Consulting Services. Led by Tim C. Mazur, Consulting Services is an internationally recognized provider of custom-designed ethics services. Our reputation for excellence is the result of helping clients directly identify and manage the *ethics* in the issues they face—rather than only legal, public relations, or similar concerns. Our team features specialists with direct experience among numerous avenues of applied ethics, including: business/workplace ethics, public service ethics, healthcare ethics, legal ethics, ethics in the professions, and ethics for nonprofit organizations.

Tim C. Mazur
Vice President
Council for Ethics in Economics
125 E. Broad Street
Columbus, OH 43215 USA
614-221-8661
614-221-8707 fax

Howard & Associates

Howard & Associates is a training organization that has been training Ethics programs around the courntry for eight years to Government, Business and Education. The course "Fairy Tales and Little White Lies" is an excellent program for organizations that want to train managers, professionals and staff on the fundamentals of ethical decision making.

Glen Howard is an excellent presenter, his training is interactive and generates a lot of discussion long after the course has ended.

Howard & Associates

P.O. Box 210
Des Moines, Iowa 50301-0210
515-274-3476
1-800-484-9719 ext. 4536
Course outline is available
references are available by request

London Research, Ltd.
  www.LondonResearch.com
  RLondon@LondonResearch.com
London Associates International
  Org. Consulting www.LondonAssocIntl.com
  Email: RWL@LondonAssocIntl.com
  Forensic Cons. www.LondonForensic.com
  Email: LF@LondonForensic.com
  Med - Arb. www.LondonMedArb.com
  Email: LMA@LondonMedArb.com
  18062 Irvine Boulevard, Suite 200
  Tustin, CA 92780-3328
  Phone 714-505-0920 / 505-0873 Fax 714-505-0874

National Inspection & Consultants, Inc. (NIC)
  NIC provides training, consulting, program development and implementation, 800 number hotline service, and investigations for ethics and employee concerns program and specializes in dealing with high profile whistleblower cases.

Janet Boulter
  I provide consulting, seminars and keynote speeches on improving business management practices through core values and high ethical standards as a means to improve profits.

Janet Boulter
3167 S. Alton Court
Denver, CO 80231
303-368-9954
303 - 368-4989- fax
e-mail: jboulter@impact-comgrp.com
www.impact-comgrp.com

Dr. R Datta, Associate Professor of Philosophy, Fayetteville State University
  Dr. R Datta, Teaches a course in Business Ethics (PHIL 430: Seminar in B. Ethics)
  Syllabus Available.
  Contact: Fay, NC 28301

Tel. 910-822-1946
Fax. . .0-630-2932
E-mail : datta@chi1.uncfsu.edu

Brailsford Consulting, Inc.
  Brailsford Counsulting, Inc. provides consultation and training for executives, managers, and employees who face ethical dilemmas when dealing with issues such as Sexual Harassment, Discrimination, Workplace Violence, Diversity, and Organizational or Strategic Change.

Patrick L. Bishop, President, **The Business Integrity Group, Inc.**
  Offering consulting services in the design of excellence and ethics within corporations, senior management training, training for U.S. Sentencing Commission Guidelines, compliance analysis and strategy development.
  Suite 1406
  241 S. 6th Street
  Philadelphia, Pennsylvania 19106-3732
  e-mail: Plbishop@aol.com
  215 829 0520

Ethical Capital
  Specializing in leadership and organizational strategies that build ethical capacity.
  Eileen Morgan, Ph.D.
  www.ethicalcapital.com

KPMG Ethics & Integrity Services

Institute for Corporate Ethics
  P O Box 1215, MESSINA 0900
  South Africa
  +27 (1553) 40619
  Stephen Mochechane
  DVEHNT1@DB.ZA
  (01554) 0272

Interactive Strategies, Inc.
  A consultancy focused on ethics and organizational culture. Analysis, research and training in relation to information collection, use and disclosure practices. Ethical action and diversity programs. Associates may be reached at: P.O. Box 5713 Station B, Victoria, B.C., Canada V8R 6S8. Please address enquiries to John J. O'Brien, C.R.M. at jobrien@access.victoria.bc.ca or voice/fax 1-250-388-7791.

Morgan-Kayhoe: Consultants to Organizations
Focusing and consulting in the area of business ethics in a global context.
58 Wells Hill Road
Weston, CT 06883
Phone: 203-454-2184, Fax: 203-221-7322
www.morgankayhoe.com
morgan@morgankayhoe.com

Navran Associates
Management Training and Consulting, speacializing in three areas: applied (business) ethics, employee empowerment and total service quality management (customer service and TQM for the service sector). They also have a special set of programs specifically for those organizations contemplating, experiencing or dealing with the aftermath of reengineering, restructuring or downsizing.

David Thrope Management Consultant to Small Business http://www1.usa1.com/~knish/dthp5.html

Professional Ethics, Inc.
A Colorado consultant organization thatprovides ethics training and education, ombudsman, ethics hotline, ethics climate survey and audit services to corporate and public sector clients. Training is tailored to the specific needs of each client organization. For information on these and other services, PEI principals can be reached at P.O. Box 136, Littleton, CO 80160, or by telephone: (719) 481-4902 /(303) 794-9568. Address inquiries to Dr. Paul Viotti, President or Warren Miller, Vice President.

Walker Tate & Associates Ethics and Law Reform Consultants.
129 Foxlow St, Captain's Flat NSW 2623, Australia. Ph/Fax: (06) 2366352. E-Mail:
mailto:wta@ozemail.com.au

Ethics Home
Site Directory | What's New?
About the Institute | Ethics Calendar
Ethics Resources | Professional Resources | Ethics Beat | DePaul Home
Comments and questions: On Ethics, lpincus@wppost.depaul.edu, or on the creation of this site, dthies@wppost.depaul.edu

Appendix III

*Samples of Organizational
Codes of Conduct*

Caux Round Table
Principles for Business
English Translation

In a world which is experiencing profound transformation, the Caux Round Table of business leaders from Europe, Japan and the United States is committed to energizing the role of business and industry as a vital force for innovative global change.

The Round Table was founded in 1986 by Frederik Philips, former President of Philips Electronics, and Olivier Giscard d'Estaing, Vice-Chairman of INSEAD, as a means of reducing escalating trade tensions. It is concerned with the development of constructive economic and social relationships between the participants' countries, and with their urgent joint responsibilities toward the rest of the world.

At the urging of Ryuzaburo Kaku, Chairman of Canon Inc., the Round Table has focused attention on the importance of global corporate responsibility in reducing social and economic threats to world peace and stability. The Round Table recognizes that shared leadership is indispensable to a revitalized and more harmonious world. It emphasizes the development of continuing friendship, understanding and cooperation, based on a common respect for the highest moral values and on responsible action by individuals in their own spheres of influence.

Introduction

The Caux Round Table believes that the world business community should play an important role in improving economic and social conditions. As a statement of aspirations, this document aims to express a world standard against which business behavior can be measured. We seek to begin a process that identifies shared values, reconciles differing values, and thereby develops a shared perspective on business behavior acceptable to and honored by all.

These principles are rooted in two basic ethical ideals: kyosei and human dignity. The Japanese concept of kyosei means living and working together for the common good enabling cooperation and mutual prosperity to coexist with healthy and fair competition. "Human dignity" refers to the sacredness or value of each person as an end, not simply as a mean to the fulfillment of others' purposes or even majority prescription.

The General Principles in Section 2 seek to clarify the spirit of kyosei and "human dignity," while the specific Stakeholder Principles in Section 3 are concerned with their practical application.

In its language and form, the document owes a substantial debt to The Minnesota Principles, a statement of business behavior developed by the Minnesota Center for Corporate Responsibility. The Center hosted and chaired the drafting committee, which included Japanese, European, and United States representatives.

Business behavior can affect relationships among nations and the prosperity and well-being of us all. Business is often the first contact between nations and, by the way in which it causes social and economic changes, has a significant impact on the level of fear or confidence felt by people worldwide. Members of the Caux Round Table place their first emphasis on putting one's own house in order, and on seeking to establish what is right rather than who is right.

DePaul's Institute for Business & Professional Ethics

Ethics WWW Resource Database
http://www.depaul.edu/ethics/codes1.html

Codes of Conduct

Illinois Institute of Technology Center for the Study of Ethics in the Professions: Codes of Ethics Online Project. For an extensive collection of codes of conduct.

The Dept. of Commerce has recently published **Model Business Principles of Business Ethics** for voluntary adoption by companies. See the latest release and guidelines.

For a small blurb on Rena Gorlin's new compilation of codes of professional responsibility and ordering information, click here.

Aseere Systems, Inc.'s Code of Ethics
   http://www.aseere-systems.com/code/
Automotive Service Association's (ASA's) Code of Ethics
   http://www.asashop.org/about/about.htm
Automotive Service Councils of California's Code of Ethics
   http://www.ascca.com/ASCGEN_f/GENMIS_f/aboutasc.htm
British Petroleum's "What We Care About" page
   http://165.121.20.76/care.html
Buckman Laboratories' Code of Ethics
   http://www.buckman.com/eng/ethics.htm
Business Exchange International's Code of Ethics
   http://sc.net/organizations/bxi/bxi-ethics.html
CCH Canadian Limited
   http://www.ca.cch.com/aboutcch/ourcomm.html
Codes of Ethics and/or Conduct
   http://web.mit.edu/afs/athena.mit.edu/org/e/ethics/www/codes.html
Codes of Ethics
   gopher://sun.bctf.bc.ca
Code of Ethics
   gopher://sunbird.usd.edu
Computer Dealers & Lessors Association
   http://www.cdla.org/cdlaethics.html
Cheney Associates' Corporate Ethical Standards
   http://www.cheney.com/ngEthics2.html
Chuck Jones & Associates, Inc.
   http://investing.com/about/ethics.htm
Ciba's Vision
   http://www.ciba.com/vision.html
Enforcing Codes of Conduct through Professional Associations
   http://www.aaas.org/spp/dspp/sfrl/per1.htm#ELPP
Halliburton Company

http://www.halliburton.com/corp/codecond/bussum.htm
Independent Cosmetic Manufacturers and Distributors, Inc.'s Membership Code of Ethics
   http://www.newmarket-forum.com/ASN/ICMAD/
International Business Brokers Association's Code of Ethics
   http://www.iea.com/~zirkle/codeeth.html
The International Ethical Business Registry
   http://www.orca.bc.ca/ethics/
International Franchise Association Code of Ethics
   http://www.mobilefranchise.com/fci/franop/ifaethic.htm
International Visual Communication Association
   http://www.webserve.co.uk/clients/ivca/ethics.htm
Johnson & Johnson's Credo
   http://www.jnj.com/credo/credo.htm
Laborers International Union of North America
   http://www.laborers.org
Lockheed Martin's "Setting the Standard: Code of Ethics and Business Conduct"
   http://www.lmco.com/exeth/
NAPA Code of Ethics
   http://csra2.csranet.com/~adnet/askaaron/ethics.htm
National Association of the Remodeling Industry (U.S.)
   http://www.bscd.com/code.htm
National Nutritional Foods Association
   http://www.melatonin.com/melnnfa1.htm
North American Bolt & Screw Co., Inc.: Values Statement
   http://www.nabs.com/nvalues.html
Northern Telecom (Nortel)
   www.nortel.com/cool/ethics/
The Rockwell Credo
   http://www.rockwell.com/rockwell/overview/credo.html
Yeo-Leong & Peh, Advocates & Solicitors' Firm's Philosophy
   http://www.singnet.com.sg/~ylplegal/phil.htm

Ethics Home
Site Directory | What's New?
About the Institute | Ethics Calendar
Ethics Resources | Professional Resources | Ethics Beat | DePaul Home
Copyright© 1997 Institute for Business and Professional Ethics. All rights reserved.

Comments and questions: On Ethics, lpincus@wppost.depaul.edu, or on the creation of this site,
dthies@wppost.depaul.edu

Appendix IV

*Print/On-Line
Magazines and Journals*

The Online Journal of Ethics

Call For Papers/Submission Guidelines

The Institute for Business & Professional Ethics is proud to announce the first online journal of business and professional ethics.

Journal Content

The Online Journal of Ethics explores both theoretical and applied ethical issues involved in the practice of business and the professions. We welcome submissions on theoretical topics such as the character and extent of social responsibility of business and the professions, the nature of the professions, and the relation between business/professional ethics and other ethics (Kantian, virtue, utilitarian, etc.). The journal will also publish papers that address pressing ethical issues in a more topical fashion. Such topics would include, e.g., the ethics of diversity training programs, downsizing initiatives, various pre-employment screening methods, empowerment, total quality management, different technologies used by corporations, and leadership, among other ideas.

Journal Online Format

The journal is an interactive mechanism which allows readers to submit comments relating to the issues presented in a particular article to the editorial staff using a submission form at the beginning of the article. Editorial staff will post comments back to the web site so that they may be read by other visitors to the site. The journal will publish two issues per year, with periodic updates to the site. It is located at:

http: //condor.depaul.edu/ethics/ethg1.html

Submissions

Submissions should be sent on disk (ds,hd) in WordPerfect format 5.1 or above, along with a hard copy, to Laura Pincus, Department of Management, DePaul University, One E. Jackson, Chicago, IL 60604. Papers should be of medium length (10-25 pp.). Authors should not use traditional legal research citations, nor footnotes or endnotes as these Wordperfect formats are not represented on the internet. Instead, please use short parenthetical references in the body of the paper, with complete references provided at the end of the paper (similar to traditional business or philosophy research references). Other code types, such as bold, underline and italics are acceptable.

Ethics Home

Site Directory | What's New?
About the Institute | Ethics Calendar
Ethics Resources | Professional Resources | Ethics Beat | DePaul Home

Comments and questions: On Ethics, lpincus@wppost.depaul.edu, or on the creation of this site, dthies@wppost.depaul.edu

Print/Magazine and Book Resources

Business Ethics
The Magazine of Socially Responsible Business

Bi-Monthly magazine for business people interested in ethics and social responsibility. Trends, company profiles, ethical case studies, management ideas, interviews, analysis of culture change, book reviews, calendar. Contains Business Ethics Network Catalogue of resources and books in socially responsible business.

52 S. 10th St. #110
Minneapolis, MN 55403-2001
612-962-4700

Business and Society Review

Quarterly journal provides insights on current corporate ethical issues, book reviews, company performance, and news on socially responsible leaders.

200 W. 57th St.
New York, NY 10019
212-399-1085

80 Exemplary Ethics Statements by Patrick E. Murphy. University of Notre Dame Press, Notre Dame, Indiana, 1998.

This book presents and comments on ethics statements from leading corporations and organizations worldwide.

Say It and Live It: The 50 Corporate Mission Statements That Hit The Mark, by Patricia Jones and Larry Kahaner, New York: Currency Doubleday, 1995.

A handbook for companies who are writing their mission statements, illustrated by the mission statements of 50 leading companies.

Playing For Keeps, by Frederick G. Harmon, New York: John Wiley & Sons, 1996.

This book looks at the relationship of a company's core values to its profitability, with steps for building a values-driven company.

Appendix V

Additional Resources

DePaul's Institute for Business & Professional Ethics

Ethics WWW Resource Database

http://www.depaul.edu/ethics/ref1.html

Links Regarding Specific Issues or Problem Areas

Landmark environmental agreement with Mitsubishi Motor Sales America, and Mitsubihsi Electric America

Radar Detectors, Fixed and Variable Costs of Crime by Timothy Stanley (Stanford University)

Pretty good discussion of the Body Shop Ethics Controversy

Whistleblowing and Trust - Some Lessons from the ADM Scandal by Daryl Koehn.

Toward Effective and Ethical Drug Abuse Prevention Policies: The Case Against Indiscriminate Drug Testing, by Robert E. Gladd, UNLV Institute for Ethics & Policy Studies

"Trust in Business"
  The Institute for Business & Professional Ethics has pictures and selected papers from our recent
  "Trust in Business" Conference
"Hard graft in Asia: business ethics"
  (survey finds that China has one of the highest rates of corruption in Asia; tips on how business
  can avoid corruption are given) from The Economist.
Global Issues: Online Poll on A Global Ethic
  http://www.rain.org/~origin/gethic/kung.html
Law & Economics Resources
  http://www.leland.stanford.edu/~tstanley/lawecon.html
Essay: The Impact of Values on Executives' Performance
  http://www.valueinsights.com/vi/impact.html
Essay: When 'good enough' is not enough
  http://www.valueinsights.com/vi/notgood.html
Enviroweb
  http://envirolink.org/
Center for Business Ethics and Environment
  http://www.nijenrode.nl:80/research/eibe.ht ml
Government, Law & Society
  http://english-www.hss.cmu.edu/Govt/
Business, Policy and Strategy
  http://comsp.com.latrobe.edu.au/bps.html
Financial/Economics World Wide Web
  http://riskweb.bus.utexas.edu:80/finweb.html
Legal-Related Information on the Web
  http://riskweb.bus.utexas.edu:80/legal.html
Organizational Issues Clearinghouse

http://haas.berkeley.edu/~seidel/ad.html
"Redefining The Corporation: An International Colloquy"
   http://www.mgmt.utoronto.ca/~stake
Municipal Bond Scandals Web Site
   http://lissack.com

Ethics Home

Site Directory | What's New?
About the Institute | Ethics Calendar
Ethics Resources | Professional Resources | Ethics Beat | DePaul Home
Copyright© 1997 Institute for Business and Professional Ethics. All rights reserved.

Comments and questions: On Ethics, lpincus@wppost.depaul.edu, or on the creation of this site,
dthies@wppost.depaul.edu

DePaul's Institute for Business & Professional Ethics

Ethics WWW Resource Database
http://www.depaul.edu/ethics/ref1.htmlhttp://www.depaul.edu/ethics/ref1.html

Business Ethics Reference-Type Resources

The Shell Report. Examples of the sort of dilemmas which managers in multinational companies are likely to face
http://www.shell.com/shellreport/pages/tell_shell_frame.html

Harvard University Program In Ethics and the Professions
http://www.harvard.com/pep

Inc. Magazine Online, site includes articles, a bulletin board, and other business ethics resources
http://www.inc.com/

A 25-page free guidebook to managing ethics in the workplace.
http://www.mapnp.org/library/ethics/ethxgde.htm

The Institute of Internal Auditors (IIA)
www.theiia.org

Baobab's Corporate Power Center, dicussing the domination of politics and culture by large corporations
http://baobabcomputing.com/corporatepower/

University of Nevada, Reno's Business Ethics Questionnaire.
http://trapeze.scs.unr.edu/~beekun/ethics/

Toward Effective and Ethical Drug Abuse Prevention Policies: The Case Against Indiscriminate Drug Testing
http://www.netcom.com/~bgladd/thesis.html

Sexual Harassment: Myths & Realities
http://www.apa.org/pubinfo/harass.html

Ethics in a Corporate Setting
http://web.mit.edu/afs/athena.mit.edu/org/e/ethics/www/corp.html

Business for Social Responsibility
http://www.bsr.org/

Council for Ethics in Economics
http://www.businessethics.org/

Better World 'Zine (BWZ)
http://www.betterworld.com/

EthicScan Canada: Consumer and Corporate Ethics Information
http://condor.depaul.edu/ethics/ethicscan.html

List of Socially Responsible Businesses
http://www.together.org:80/srb/bizlist.html

Ethical and Social Business Directory
http://www.bath.ac.uk:80/Centres/Ethical/

Socially Responsible Businesses in the United States
http://www.together.org:80/srb/

Social Issues in Management Directory and International Association for Business & Society Network

http://cac.psu.edu/~plc/iabs.html- Listerver at: listserv@psuvm.psu.edu
List of Business Schools On-Line
   http://www.yahoo.com/Business/Bu siness_Schools/
   http://www.sloan.mit.edu/useful/otherB.html
   Review of b-school sites: http://www.clemson.edu/~marm/bus.html
Ethical Investment Research Service
   http://www.u-net.com:80/~gaeia/gaeiaers.htm
Antitrust, ethics and mortgage discrimination (Home page withrelated research papers)
   http://www.pub.utdallas.edu/~liebowit/
Socially Responsible Business Forum
   http://www.srb.org/forum/
Resources available to economists on the Web
   http://econwpa.wustl.edu/EconFAQ/EconFAQ.html
Meta-Index for Non-profit Organizations
   http://www.ai.mit.edu/people/ellens/non-meta.html
Canadian Ethical Investment Guide
   http://www.web.apc.org/ethmoney/
Social Issues in Management
   http://cac.psu.edu/~plc/iabs.html
Business Ethics Listserver
   Contact: William Baumer
Berkeley Students for Responsibile Business
   http://hass.berkeley.edu/~asutton/srbb.html
Berkeley Students for Responsibile Business
   http://dolphin.upenn.edu/~mba_wsrb/
Virtual Law Library Reference Desk
   http://law.wuacc.edu/washlaw/reflaw/reflaw.html
The National Debt Clock (click on "reload" once you get there for a second-by-second update!)
   http://www.brillig.com/debt_clock/
Additional Law Guides and Resource Lists
   http://www.law.cornell.edu/index.html
The Legallist
   ftp://ftp.midnight.com/ go to: pub/Legallist/Legallist.txt
Long list of other Gopher resources
   gopher://liberty.uc.wlu.edu:3002/7?ethics
Public Administration **Listserver** to discuss ethics issues, dilemmas, decision making and
teaching/training approaches.
   email listserv@nosferatu.cas.usf.edu, leave subject line open and type in body: SUBSCRIBE
   ETHTALK-L (your name)
St. Ambrose University Business Ethics Site
   http://www.sau.edu/cwis/internet/wild/majors/Business/BusEthic/beindex.html
DEMOS
   http://www.cityscape.co.uk/users/fj22/busethpr.htm
Finance and Commerce Information Services
   http://www.finance-commerce.com/fcpg1.htm

Index

Page references followed by "f" denote figures

Butterworth-Heinemann Business Books . . .
for Transforming Business

5th Generation Management, Co-creating Through Virtual Enterprising, Dynamic Teaming, and Knowledge Networking, Revised Edition,
Charles M. Savage, 0-7506-9701-6

Beyond Strategic Vision: Effective Corporate Action with Hoshin Planning,
Michael Cowley and Ellen Domb, 0-7506-9843-8

Beyond Time Management: Business with Purpose,
Robert A. Wright, 0-7506-9799-7

The Breakdown of Hierarchy: Communicating in the Evolving Workplace,
Eugene Marlow and Patricia O'Connor Wilson, 0-7056-9746-6

Business and the Feminine Principle: The Untapped Resource,
Carol R. Frenier, 0-7506-9829-2

Cultivating Common Ground: Releasing the Power of Relationships at Work,
Daniel S. Hanson, 0-7506-9832-2

Flight of the Phoenix: Soaring to Success in the 21st Century,
John Whiteside and Sandra Egli, 0-7506-9798-9

Getting a Grip on Tomorrow: Your Guide to Survival and Success in the Changed World of Work,
Mike Johnson, 0-7506-9758-X

Innovation Strategy for the Knowledge Economy: The Ken Awakening,
Debra M. Amidon, 0-7506-9841-1

The Intelligence Advantage: Organizing for Complexity,
Michael D. McMaster, 0-7506-9792-X

The Knowledge Evolution: Expanding Organizational Intelligence,
Verna Allee, 0-7506-9842-X

Leadership in a Challenging World: A Sacred Journey,
Barbara Shipka, 0-7506-9750-4

Leading from the Heart: Choosing Courage over Fear in the Workplace,
Kay Gilley, 0-7506-9835-7

Learning to Read the Signs: Reclaiming Pragmatism in Business,
F. Byron Nahser, 0-7506-9901-9

Marketing Plans that Work: Targeting Growth and Profitability,
Malcolm H.B. McDonald and Warren J. Keegan, 0-7506-9828-4

A Place to Shine: Emerging from the Shadows at Work,
Daniel S. Hanson, 0-7506-9738-5

Power Partnering: A Strategy for Business Excellence in the 21st Century
Sean Gadman, 0-7506-9809-8

Resources for the Knowledge-Based Economy Series

> *Knowledge Management and Organizational Design,*
> Paul S. Myers, 0-7506-9749-0
>
> *Knowledge Management Tools,*
> Rudy L. Ruggles, III, 0-7506-9849-7
>
> *Knowledge in Organizations,*
> Laurence Prusak, 0-7506-9718-0
>
> *The Strategic Management of Intellectual Capital,*
> David A. Klein, 0-7506-9850-0

Setting the PACE® in Product Development: A Guide to Product And Cycle-time
> *Excellence,*
Michael E. McGrath, 0-7506-9789-X

Time to Take Control: The Impact of Change on Corporate Computer Systems,
Tony Johnson, 0-7506-9863-2

The Transformation of Management,
Mike Davidson, 0-7506-9814-4

Who We Could Be at Work, Revised Edition,
Margaret A. Lulic, 0-7506-9739-3

To purchase a copy of any Butterworth-Heinemann Business title, please visit
your local bookstore or call 1-800-366-2665.

Eileen Morgan brings nearly two decades of experience working in diverse global companies to her consulting firm *Morgan-Kayhoe: Consultants to Organizations,* an organization development and management consulting firm based in Weston, CT and Keene, NH. As an organization consultant, Eileen's work centers on large systems change efforts in major corporations and focuses specifically on building organizational capacity for competence and confidence. She is most interested in consulting with clients around organizational issues of business and ethics in global companies, where leadership, values, cross-cultural, and organizational development issues converge. She is the founder of Ethical Capital, a consulting company helping global companies increase their capacity for ethical organizational behavior.

Eileen Morgan earned her Ph.D. in Human and Organizational Systems from The Fielding Institute, holds an M.A. in Organization Development, and an M.S. in Counseling. When not travelling the globe for personal or business reasons, she enjoys a quiet life in the Weston, Connecticut countryside with her partner, Keith Melville.

To learn more about Eileen's work visit the following websites:

www.ethicalcapital.com

www.morgankayhoe.com